I0004272

Artificial Intelligence in Short

Ryan Richardson Barrett

Published by Ryan Richardson Barrett, 2024.

ARTIFICIAL INTELLIGENCE IN SHORT

First edition. February 14, 2024.

Written by Ryan Richardson Barrett.
Book Cover Design by ebooklaunch.com

Table of Contents

For my grandparents Dewey and Shirley.

I want to thank my parents for their support, and I would also like to express gratitude to my friends, Brandon, Cole, Chris, Craig, Emily, Matthew, McDiesel, Patrick, and Timothy, for their encouragement.

Introduction

Artificial intelligence (AI) is enhancing the logic of computer programs. Logic has multiple meanings. One meaning of logic is the syntax and structure of computer code and its structure. The second meaning of logic involves the word's more well-known definition, which describes acts of reasoning intended to consider outcomes that are good, bad, or both. Logic is important in the context of artificial intelligence and coincides with AI's purpose: to assist machines in acting logically. Machine learning (ML) is enhancing the processes of learning uniquely used by machines. Outlining ideas and planning what to do in the future is how people make sound decisions. Computer programs that feature machine learning have similar, yet simpler, processes. Machine learning programs have layers of steps they take before arriving at an objectively reasoned conclusion and are tuned to reproduce certain results. More elaborate ML applications have deeper layers of logic.

Machine learning was reorganized in the 1990s from other realms of computer science. Computer programming languages like Ruby, Python, Java, and others gave developers the necessary toolkits to implement machine learning techniques and algorithms into code. After the reorganization, ML was affirmed to be capable of implementing probability and statistics into computer applications to improve functionality. Increased effectiveness was the reason for embedding machine learning algorithms into programming code.

The term AI is regularly used to denote a specific machine learning model or computer application that acts intelligently. An example of such usage would be to say that Chat GPT-4 is AI. AI exists in many different forms. However, all forms of AI mimic intelligent behavior, which is remarkable because humans frequently show intelligent behavior. Humans are easily able to look around a room and recognize objects. Humans can even sometimes discern the purpose of an object without having previously encountered that unknown thing. Humans can look at things with wings, like a bird or a plane, and determine if they can fly. Using past experiences to understand and predict the future is how humans make decisions, and AI's logic attempts to follow that human formula. However, humans understand context while machines struggle with that complicated process.

Modern software can identify a huge number of objects in digital images. Unlike people, software can only rely on datasets to recognize objects in an image. Machine learning software lacks cognition and fails to solve problems in nuanced ways. On the contrary, humans have a much broader skill set in problem-solving than AI. Narrow artificial intelligence, which is AI that can complete certain specific tasks, is the main form of AI. General artificial intelligence, by contrast, matches the capabilities of a human by being able to interact with any number of problems and can accomplish elaborate tasks, although general AI does not yet exist.

Despite hindered intellect (by human standards), AI can be extremely creative. The extent of extremeness occasionally produces concepts no human has ever considered, which is frequently a result of mathematical algorithms rapidly executing. The Magic 8 Ball was created as a toy that produced decisions. Although artificial, the toy is not encouragingly intelligent. However, dice-roll decision making, or making the decision probabilistic in the case of the 8 Ball by way of its twenty different responses, can yield interesting results in both cases. AI can present an inhuman creativity in finding solutions to problems. The Magic 8 Ball's twenty responses pale in comparison to large language model (LLM) chatbots and their countless possible responses to input. Randomness resembles creativity. AI is creating new algorithms and is excellent at exploring patterns amidst vast data.

The five senses, sight, smell, touch, hearing, and taste have greatly contributed to what programmers focus on pursuing when AI models are developed. Of course, not all of the senses are tangible for a computer to currently create interactions with. Human perception is intended to be imitated by machines when designing AI-based applications. Cameras suffice as mechanical vision, and microphones intercept vibrations much like the cochlea of the inner ear does. Computer vision (CV) is a recent innovation in computer technology. Computer vision is the name given to machine learning models that evaluate or otherwise use images. One common task of CV is to identify and label objects seen in an image. By evaluating patterns, similarities in color, and the geometrical edges of an image, machine learning will compare similarly databased objects, and if the tested image resembles known images, the computer vision program will have used its learnings to see and recognize.

Artificial intelligence began as a philosophical term that refers to how humans try to recreate their own methods of making intelligent decisions. Intelligent decisions, in this case, require a combination of rapid critical thinking while using memories from the past to make thoughtful decisions in real time. ML is the mechanization of how machines imitate human-like methods of learning, but the methods ML models use are significantly simpler than the human brain. An argument could also be made that machine learning models use more algorithms and expressions from probability than a human would make when deciding what stores to go and shop at or other typical decisions people make in their daily lives.

The mathematics used by machine learning models act as a bonus skill artificially intelligent systems can use to solve problems in ways human thinking would struggle to do quickly or fail to do altogether. Calculations that software completes are computed almost instantly. A computer can run formulas that accept an input and then produce an output, usually aided my mathematical equations often from the branch of linear algebra. Due to the computation speed of computers, mathematics can produce objectively good decisions when integrated into computer code. When people play darts, players do not think of the numerical degrees at which the dart is thrown. Good dart players operate on feel, which is a result of repetition and technique they have practiced in the sport. Humanlike methods combined with formulaic steps often work the best when solving significant puzzles. The puzzles AI solves are simply referred to as tasks.

A person cannot combine several images to make a new image as fast as the CV model Stable Diffusion can. If a human were to attempt the same feat, achieving the desired effect would take hours at best, while Stable Diffusion can produce images in seconds. Later in the book, CV models will be extensively discussed.

One method of classifying AI is by what the AI model does. Furthermore, artificial intelligence models are also referred to as networks in some cases because AI models can have multiple tiers or blocks of logic in the application that work together, thus forming a system of computer functions, which fits closely to the definition of a network, particularly in computer science and neuroscience. Artificial neural networks (ANN) are a method of loosely imitating the structure of the brain. AI models primarily focus on images or language. ML is also involved in uses that relate to sound. Sound waves are displayed by images, and those same images are what machine learning models classify and evaluate so that the system can recognize what a sound is or, in the case of generative AI, make new sounds or even songs.

Classification is a critical component of machine learning. In ML's realm of study, a classifier determines a piece of data's respective place. Data is categorized into different groups in which the group shares similar properties. Classification grows more specific as machine learning layers increase in depth. A computer vision model that evaluates images to search for people's faces would need to have a prerequisite at different blocks, blocks being the levels of code that make up the AI model. The first block would need to determine characteristics that all faces share.

Artificial intelligence and deep learning (DL) have made incredible progress in the last decade. Since the birth of the concept of AI in 1950 by Alan Turing, AI has become far more practical after successive generational improvements in computer science. Although cognitive psychology theorizes concepts of human thought, computer science creates functioning examples of these ideas. Artificial intelligence is a concept that has grown to mean more than its name entails. Recent innovations in CPU (central processing unit) and GPU (graphics processing unit) technology have increased computational power in both types of common computer chips. Additionally, tensor processing units are becoming more commonplace when AI testing requires computational assistance that exceeds what a CPU and GPU could provide. Increases in the storage drive size of computers have allowed AI systems to function better. AI applications usually require a significant amount of storage and processing power so the system can run operations promptly, especially during the model's training.

The use of AI is becoming integral to many applications, specifically search engines. Machine learning is being incorporated into core device applications. Common applications using ML techniques are increasing as palpable improvements are simultaneously flourishing in ML strategies. Artificial intelligence's practicality is supreme to its initially conceptualist ideals. The effects of artificial intelligence have begun to alter international legislature, dramatically impact technology companies, and make computer software function at a higher level of capability. AI implemented into technology makes technology function more efficiently, especially when people understand how to assist AI, as its use cases are hindered by mediocre datasets and a lack of human-like reasoning. AI models require good datasets and real-world rationale from their creators in order to be developed.

The 1980s was a generation of common literary discussion about AI, then the fad faded away, but progress did not stop. Several times, AI and similar concepts have become popular, then slowly waned. The 1980s wave of artificial intelligence progress was spurred on by better computing power from CPUs. Today, the broad-reaching discussion regarding intelligence and software has been encouraged by numerous successful uses of AI and deep learning to complete many tasks better than a person can. Deep learning is an integral concept related to AI and refers to how more logic layers built into an ML platform increase complexity and purported depth. Numerous common formats of technology have implemented AI mechanisms; using a personal computer or smartphone now relies on AI technologies for many social media sites, word processing applications, and facial recognition as a means of verification in security. Deep learning applications have extended beyond intelligence and made progress in becoming creative, leading to improvements in scientific fields that use images and language. Patterns uncovered by algorithmic learning have brought significant benefits to efficiency and the scope of problems software can solve.

ML is critical to AI and is AI's mechanism of action. Applications are frequently given data that they will then utilize, although most machine learning applications can improve upon an outcome specified by a human supervisor. Machines are currently incapable of intuition, and the neural networks of mammalian brains are significantly more complicated than artificial neural networks.

Applications that use deep learning are taught similarly to how people are instructed. People learn things in structured ways, like witnessing repetitive occurrences. When things happen frequently, surely frequency can begin to be predicted. However, both people and machines can also learn by experience, which involves trial and error. People have memories they keep for the rest of their lives, and these memories have a big influence on their decision-making. Old form factor applications are contained within themselves, and all their code uses the traditional aspects of coding syntax. Numerous applications do not require AI models to complete their purpose because some computer applications need to be simple and do not require elaborate layered ML algorithms in their code.

The usage of datasets is the most notable difference between a typical application and an AI-integrated application. Applications that function with the assistance of machine learning are provided directions and formatted data the application can utilize. ML algorithms sort data and learn the data's features. Traditional applications do not store information to change new processes. In many cases, AI applications utilize human input to improve decision-making. AI can create algorithms that result in a certain outcome, but the developers must decide what the outcome should resemble. Data science directly interacts with deep learning because unstructured data can be sorted by machine learning to create labels in a process called self-supervision. A consistent pattern of an ML application is that the software can recognize patterns in data; thus, the software is a machine in the process of learning –a phrase that describes more than a brief thought would suggest.

Examples of artificial intelligence platforms using machine learning are powerful and provide a substantial show of strength when it comes to visualizations, but they also have effective impacts on what modern technology can do. The impacts of artificial intelligence, with the involvement of biological intelligence, are pushing progress forward in technology once again. The principles of artificial intelligence provide a few notable goals, but the most important is the ability of a computer to resemble human-like behavior, if only in a minute way; Turing did well to instantiate this concept. Artificial intelligence originated as a hypothetical idea, but today, technology is more effective than it was in the past, thus enabling rapid progress in the field. Deep learning has been placed into situations where it may not have been initially thought to have practical use, like in medicine and chemistry, and produced incredible results. People are looking for help from AI.

Chapter 1 – Practical AI

To further elaborate on Alan Turing's concepts, in 1950, Turing staged an experiment where he had participants communicate with a person and a machine. The participant was limited to using text to communicate, and both human and machine correspondents could only use text when they would send and receive replies. If the participant could not specify which line of communication was the machine, the machine would then pass the Turing test (Turing, 1950). AI applications, if successful, generally pass the Turing test and can be impossible to discern from a person's creations, especially in text communication and visual forms of AI. Practical AI applications use modern technology to make the most of Turing's thought-provoking ideas. However, AI has moved beyond scientific experimentation and has become common in computer programming.

Artificial intelligence conceptualizes and enables machines to function in a way that resembles human thinking; however, it only describes the loose category to which software adheres. DL and ML techniques more clearly outline how a computer system adapts and changes to complete a task or solve a problem. A common visual showcasing for machine learning systems uses software to maneuver a virtual 3D character that learns how to walk forward around obstacles (Warehouse, 2023). The character model struggles through hundreds of attempts before the proper algorithms are discovered and then used to enable the walker to stroll forward.

ML can use trial and error methods, which is especially useful in finding paths or streamlining other tedious processes. Not all solutions are known, and the ability of machine learning to occur requires repetition. ML systems take in data and use algorithms to organize the data for different uses, such as classification or predictions. As more data moves through the algorithm, the system improves, and thus, the model appears to be learning. Concepts of AI's initial configuration and how AI is taught and learns will be covered in this chapter.

Machine Learning

ML allows a machine to organize data into categories so features can be determined. Features have a unique meaning when used in ML and are the patterns and other similarities in data ML learns. Classification is a core component of machine learning because ML-integrated applications must note features in data. Finding similarities among data is as important as finding dissimilar features in the data an ML model evaluates. Data classification and unsupervised machine learning are closely linked. Data that is disorganized will need to be classified. People have trouble classifying millions of objects rapidly, while AI does not. Classifying data can show how different ranges of data are clustered together and, therefore, how the data is related to its specific group. Noting features in data determines common aspects of things. For example, when CV evaluates images of lightbulbs, a common feature of all lightbulbs is that many of the pixels in the images have the same proportional shape; there are only so many types of lightbulbs. AI processes data in steps frequently referred to as layers. The edge lines that show a lightbulb, or in other words, the cropped-out perimeter of a lightbulb, is the CV strategy of how shapes are learned in image datasets. Some AI models can use overarching (called global) requirements to speed up computation by stopping unnecessary layers from making null calculations that are not helpful.

Algorithms in the source code of ML programs are strategies for helping an AI application learn. A machine is considered to have learned when the system improves at a task after receiving data. The programmed structure of an AI model and the algorithms the model uses are what separates different types of models. AI models can use the same datasets but produce different results because of their dissimilar operations. However, models usually specialize in handling a certain type of data. Some artificially intelligent models make unique algorithms to help sort data, while others are pretrained for a certain use case. Later, specific models of AI will be explained in conjunction with their purpose.

A simple way to classify data is to remove data that exists as outliers. To provide an example, a theoretical large language model creates summaries of large groups of text, such as books or short stories. The task of the theoretical model is to summarize the text. One method to make a summary is to combine similar sentences. The model is only intended to summarize and shorten the story; in doing so, a cutoff must be set so the summaries are short and precise. When the model searches through the story, longer sentences might cause problems for the algorithms to evaluate. Long sentences are too elaborate and contain complex words like adjectives and adverbs that are unimportant to the summary. To prevent the model from creating errors, a limit of twenty words needs to be set for sentence length that can be input into the model. If the model comes across a sentence longer than twenty words, the sentence will be ignored and will not contribute to the summary. Of course, a more advanced program could summarize longer text, but this example shows the robustness of simplicity when using ML strategies.

Deep Learning

Having an initial check for word length is an example of one of the many blocks of code a DL system may have. These blocks can also be called nodes when referred to in the context of artificial neural networks, a type of deep learning that takes inspiration from the structure of neurons in the brain but with significantly simpler connections. The brain's neurons have less depth than some deep learning models but far more width, so to speak. Deep learning uses different algorithms to manipulate the data that has been input into the system. Layers of code allow deep learning applications to make more complicated evaluations.

DL networks are named as such because the networks include multiple mathematical functions combined with other types of computer decisions to verify an outcome. Not all deep learning algorithms are comprised of neural networks, but neural networking is one of the most advanced strategies in structuring logic into a computer program. The structure of the brain was the initial inspiration for neural networks, but in today's world, the implementations are different in each respective network. Despite the implications of the name, deep learning is not a direct imitation of the cognition enabled by a brain –specifically, a highly intelligent mammalian brain. If the field of neuroscience understood the brain better than the current state of science permits, deep learning would still deviate from the exact processes of how brains function. Artificial neurons usually communicate in one direction, except in recurrent neural networks, which can flow forward or backward in different ways when moving information among nodes. Biological neurons have complex connections, frequently more than one or two, that communicate in several ways that are still being studied.

Deep learning systems can use multiple server computers in succession to assist in processing at an enterprise level. Connected groups of servers are networks. The congruent nature of the network allows different machines and their GPUs in the network to communicate together. In neural networks, virtual nodes communicate with one another, whereas in physical server infrastructure, servers, network storage boxes, and personal computers communicate together. Enterprise-level AI applications made by companies like OpenAI, Google's various subsidiaries, Microsoft, and other tech corporations use custom servers and daisy-chained GPUs to train AI models.

Defining what ML is not is just as important as defining what ML is. In practical use, classification is one of the first tasks an algorithm will complete. Evaluating an image or collection of words, which are tasks of CV and large language models respectively, is one of the first steps in classification. The words and images are placed into metaphorical boxes, and depending on the categories the evaluated data adheres to, the data can be understood by the model. Using the word understood recognizes the model's ability to improve at the task it has been assigned to complete. This level of understanding is finite and not highly accurate. Computer applications that do not learn and do not improve from repetitive ingestion of data are not artificially intelligent.

Artificial Neural Networks

ANNs establish decision-making by clustering neurons. Simulated neural networks (SNNs) are machine learning networks that have nodes that communicate within the network. A node is a component in a neural network and has an engineered purpose. Connectionism is a term that originated in the 1930s after concepts of how the human brain functions were detailed in a mathematical and quantifiable way (Buckner & Garson, 2019). Connectionism is the study of connected neurons communicating together, which further elaborates on synthetic and biological neural network's function. The more functions added, the more depth is gained. With depth comes complexity but also better outputs that are closer to the desired outcome. In an ANN, different neurons can be focused which is the concept of attention. Weighting different variables, which is assigning a level of importance to certain neurons or layers, helps determine a hierarchy of importance when it comes to recognizing features. In image classification, using color as a highly weighted variable can help in determining species of birds, for example. An image of a cardinal must contain red, albeit in different shades. Red would be a necessary feature for affirming an image is of a cardinal and is a specific heavily weighted variable.

Generalization is a machine learning model's ability to perform classification or other types of evaluations on data that has not been trained for but is still similar enough to be examined. Images being larger or smaller could potentially have impacts on how the images are classified, but a robust model would not have issues being able to accept differently sized images. Training and supervision are substantial contributors to how well an AI model can generalize. Too little training can cause the system to fail to recognize important common features. Too much training can result in the system effectively memorizing the data on which it was trained. Rote memorization causes issues during machine and human learning. Real-world applications do not provide a perfect fit for algorithms, which is why they need to avoid being trained to match one limited set of data.

In probability, the method commonly known as nearest neighbor (or k-nearest neighbor) searching is a way ML can solve problems with minimal supervision. The nearest neighbor algorithm is one of ML's most commonly used algorithms. Nearest neighbor functions can help discover the most efficient routes to a destination when certain stops must be made along the way, hence its reference to neighborhoods. An employee of a pizza restaurant follows practices similar to this concept. When delivering pizzas, the delivery person goes to places that are closest as they make their stops. The driver does not randomly travel across town; they continue to go to the next closest delivery destination. Rather than traveling to destinations randomly, nearest neighbor algorithms will find the next closest point of interest.

Decision Trees

Decision trees are outlines or pathways for how decisions can be made. Decision trees start with an initial decision, the root node, and are imagined as the roots of a tree. Extending from the root node are internal nodes, of which there can be many. Internal nodes contain subsequent logic. However, only a specific pathway can be chosen. Following the selection of an internal node, a leaf node will also be selected to arrive at the end of the leaves and at the final decision. Staying consistent with this concept's tree analogy, pruning is used to remove nonrelevant branches that training has proven to be non-valuable. Levels of analysis are frequently represented in decision trees. Various mathematical functions can be placed into certain branches of decision trees to analyze data inserted into the algorithm with further complexity.

Having a large portion of unused branches can make training less effective and require more computational power. When a model processes numerous decisions, even if they are determined to quickly continue to the next node, skipping the decision is faster than determining a null answer. Delays in a model producing results delay training and can decrease the overall function of the model.

There is a general prerequisite to DL's structure: the model needs to contain three or more layers of logic. Deep learning models use neural networks to great effect and vary in depth and complexity. Given enough data, deep learning applications can make extremely nuanced decisions by having multiple levels of logic. The large language model Chat GPT-3 has one hundred seventy-five billion nodes due to how it handles individual words (Brown et al., 2020). Chat GPT-4 certainly has even more nodes, although the developers of Chat GPT (OpenAI) have not specified how many.

Deep learning exists as a group of nodes organized into hierarchies. The most important nodes interact with data at the highest levels before moving on to less significant ways to evaluate a piece of data. The hierarchies work together to attain information about the data that is fed into the system. With time, data, and experience, an ML model can be trained to be more nuanced and start to become more generalized in use. However, there is a ceiling for how well a model can operate; models do not continue to improve indefinitely, and overtraining causes issues.

Reinforcement learning is a significant highlight of the achievements of deep learning. Reinforcement learning allows a deep learning model to repeat a task independently to find an optimal way of completing the task. Independent operation of an ML system is a critical goal of artificial intelligence, and functioning without human assistance could help find new ways for computer systems to solve problems that human cognition struggles with. Several pre-trained AI models are available for public use. Once a model has been trained, the models can manage new situations and maintain their coded logic for use with other datasets.

Decision trees are a simple learning algorithm that works well for uses that require minimum overhead. Treed decisions work best in simple scenarios with small numbers of nodes. Adding too many branches wastes computer processing resources. To continue to the next branch is the ultimate decision each nexus or branch of a tree can make, which refines the simplicity of this type of algorithm. Still, using a probability or algebraic function will frequently be more effective than a decision tree due to the resulting quantifiable result (Pedregosa et al., 2011). Probability calculations in machine learning yield a specific number that allows better classifications. With better classifications come better predictions and more advanced ML capabilities.

Computer science occasionally borrows techniques from biology, and synthetic neural networks are not the only example. Evolutionary computation is a fascinating facet of computer science that incorporates ideas of evolutionary change into computer models. Machine learning uses evolutionary computation by creating an initial output solution and making tiny incremental changes to the solution to create a better outcome (Dumitrescu et al., 2000). Supervision frequently assists the system in making sure the desired outcome is clearly outlined. Not all new generations created by evolutionary computation are close to the outcome desired by the model. If a useless outcome is produced, the outcome is removed, and another variation is attempted. As evolutionary computation produces more outcomes, a high level of accuracy can be achieved. This form of learning is very effective when methods of completing a task are known but in desperate need of improvement.

Seeing Software

A machine learning algorithm can be instructed to find a certain number of clusters in a dataset. Clustering is when unsupervised ML models organize data into certain groups. ML models can cluster data based on density or other similarities the data has, like numerical similarities. Clustering and classification work in tandem. After clustering, the data can be labeled or organized. The problem with such a request is that the number of appropriate clusters is hard to know. Data clustering is very important in CV and most fields of AI. For computer vision tasks, colors need to be classified. Blue has multiple different values. However, at some point, the color value is no longer blue. When a computer vision application labels ranges of blue pixels, an algorithm would need to run to determine the parts of an image that fit the ranges of blue that appear most commonly in the dataset. During training, a computer vision model could be fed pictures of the ocean. If the model is intended to label oceans and other bodies of water in an image, an important feature to note is the colors that bodies of water contain. Once the program flows through checking parameters, pixels in an image fall into the range of colors regarded as being a possible body of water. Afterward, other nodes can be made to improve verification that certain features indicate a body of water being present in the image.

Other classifications are made for images as well. Shapes and edge lines can be copied from an image by using a type of overlapping filter (Jain et al., 1995). Identifying shapes can help vision programs evaluate images for items like traffic signs. The octagonal shape of a stop sign helps people to recognize the sign, even when the sign may be obscured by poor weather or debris and brush concealing the sign. Few objects in day-to-day life are octagon-shaped, making recognition of the edge lines of a stop sign an easy task for CV. The eight angles inside of an octagon are each 135 degrees; seeing just one or two rare 135-degree angles on the roadside could help a computer vision system recognize a stop sign. Other road signs can be triangular, such as the warning signs for animals like deer, bears, or squirrels. These signs can also be classified by their shape. Further evaluation needs to be made by an AI model before deducing that all things shaped like an octagon or triangle are truly traffic signs. Many road signs also have images or other color patterns in the sign to help drivers achieve rapid recognition when it is difficult to read the words on a sign. The blocks of a computer vision AI model might evaluate road signs in the following order: shape (edge lines), colors, and words (edge lines inside of a shape). A group of researchers were able to recognize eighty different objects using the computer vision models Open CV and YOLO (you only look once) (Reddy et al., 2023). The number of items identifiable by different CV models is increasing as datasets grow and improve in image quality, which assists ML in finding more subtle features.

Computer vision programs 'see' things and make evaluations of the objects. However, AI goes about tasks in more analytical ways than a person. AI finds patterns in the visual world where humans may not. Human drivers make decisions specific to certain situations. Drivers may not stop at all stop signs, especially if they are familiar with the intersection –general chaos at play. Signs on a highway that show there is a traffic light ahead, which signals a driver to reduce their speed, can also be noted by the traffic lights themselves or an increase in traffic congestion in the area. A multitude of other more subtle hints exist on roads that human drivers rapidly notice. Automated driving systems powered by AI must incorporate several different datasets to reference when processing visual circumstances on the road. A lack of datasets negatively affects the current practicality of autonomous driving. Rapidly changing situations hinder AI's ability to make improvements over time because the tasks change quickly while driving.

Computer science was in its infancy when Turing first conducted his experiments. The field has grown to incorporate Turing's ideas, and the man has had a tremendous influence on concepts of AI as well as computer science. LLMs, some of which are colloquially referred to as chatbots, epitomize artificial intelligence by causing users to experience an uncanny feeling. Having a conversation with software is a strange experience. Generative AI, which is software that can create things using machine learning algorithms, does not just create simple sentences and phrases but can also create images and sounds. Chatbots implement generative AI to create new text by combining known texts. The method of creation varies depending on which AI model is used, but usually generative AI combines different forms of data (like text or sounds) to create something new.

Large Language Models

Language models respond in an average manner. Combining likely responses from datasets yields results that usually have few outliers. In other words, the way LLMs produce responses is not very creative or unique, but the answers they provide are frequently reasonable, if not somewhat inaccurate. Therefore, language models are a great resource for producing text documents and can translate languages. If you ask a chatbot a complex problem, the system will give an average answer, even if the question warrants a more elaborate response. Chatbots combine information from sources and structure the responses based on how commonly words are placed together, a less-than-ideal method of writing. The ruse a chatbot maintains is dissimilar from other interactions a person can have with technology. Being able to maintain a discussion with AI is interesting and one of the best ways to interact with artificial intelligence. Unlike LLMs, generative images made by AI can be created in visually beautiful ways despite using similar average algorithms. The fact that an image of a person can be created from computer vision models and that image is nearly indecipherable from an actual photo of a person shows the effects of AI's consistency. Generative CV has completely nullified people's practical effectiveness in being able to view an image and assume it is a genuine digital photograph. AI image generation is starting to achieve realism at an incredible pace.

Language translation tasks, such as translating English into Spanish or into a language like Mandarin Chinese that has completely different characters than English, have become faster and more accurate when LLMs get involved with natural language processing. Language differences, such as slang or usage of words with varying definitions, can make accurate translation difficult. Many languages are not well documented, and most translations rely on texts that state the same material in varying languages (Caswell & Bapna, 2022). Incorporating large language models into language translation has helped create translations that use words commonly structured together in a sentence.

Artificial intelligence can be very convincing. To continue to elaborate on how AI is created to engage with the five senses, AI also can create, as well as manipulate, images. DALL-E can create images of people and other complex things, some of which look as though they are fairly normal digital photographs. The collection of images DALL-E relies on to create new images has grown substantially, and with that dataset growth comes better image creation.

AI video creation is rapidly making progress towards video that is as believable and as well-made as AI images. Images created with CV have improved rapidly in the last six months. If generated videos are anything like images, only a few months to years will pass before that technology achieves the ability to pass the Turing test. Vision is one of the most capable human senses machines must imitate to interact in a human-centered world.

The ability of artificial intelligence applications to create a sense of realism is a fundamental goal of AI. Elaborate applications exist for AI, and modern research is exploring using AI as a solution to many problems in fields such as medicine, business, and data science. To understand AI, one must comprehend machine learning because machine learning (namely deep learning) has allowed programmers to make applications that resemble intelligent systems that can learn, albeit with limitations and significant human assistance. Deep learning has become one of the leading methods of computer learning. Deep learning applications are effective.

Supervised Learning and Training

Supervised training is the name given to the assistance of AI so that it may improve its decision-making with human help. Supervised learning, named from the machine's perspective, requires data to be specifically labeled before the ML model can ingest it. Some machine learning models are intended to be used without supervision. If the ML system does not require supervision, it is considered unsupervised, and those processes do not attain ideal algorithms quickly. Standard machine learning can be unsupervised in its pursuit of discerning features. Unsupervised systems are also more complicated than supervised in terms of development and training time. Unsupervised learning is not perfectly literal in most cases. During unsupervised learning, aspects of data are noted typically by classifying or otherwise categorizing aspects of the dataset the model has been tasked with analyzing. The main goal of this analysis is to give a consensus on the characteristics of the data.

All data has features, with more data leading to more easily learned features. Representation learning is the summarization of patterns to discover aspects of the data. Representation learning and feature learning are different names for the same thing. The way representation learning functions is by taking high-dimensional data and sorting the data into a lower dimension (Bengio et al., 2013). A similar way to think about representational learning is simplifying complicated data and finding parts that can be more directly understood. Not all types of data are easy to use; data can be noisy, with many useless features that distract machine learning processes. ML algorithms find ways to represent data at different dimensionalities. The representations of data are a good starting point in labeling a dataset and can even assist the ML algorithm to become self-supervised. The sorting enabled by representational learning saves time.

The primary distinction between supervised and unsupervised learning is whether the data that the model evaluates is labeled. A label is usually made of a few words attached to a piece of data, such as an image or text. Labels do not exist for some datasets, and it can be much easier for an ML model to create labels than a person. Self-supervised learning creates labels as data is ingested. Self-supervised is usually the most advanced and complex type of supervision.

Semi-supervised learning and other types of supervision take place as machines learn. Reinforcement learning (RL) is when a system interacts with an unknown environment. The system must make decisions that are conducive to a certain type of success. The repetition of the learned protocol leads to improvements. The system affirms that the decisions it makes are recognized as appropriate, and therefore, decisions that work towards the desired outcome are reinforced. Reinforcement learning is an excellent model for completing complicated tasks that do not have a set formula for success but an understood desired outcome. The RL model's job is to find the best way to succeed. Reinforcement allows an ML model to produce ways of completing a task faster, if not better in its entirety, than what a human could produce.

Supervised learning algorithms are given an input that is then mapped to an output. Supervised learning also uses labeled data that adheres to a certain format. Other formatting requirements could be that images must be within certain dimensions that cannot exceed a specified size. Forcing the system to match the input to a set output allows an algorithm to be created that will continue to attribute slight variations in input as being the same general data that needs to be organized. Learning algorithms are important to train properly so that they can deny truly invalid input but still utilize a broad range of input data. If an algorithm can only accept an extremely limited range of data, the model will not be practical for use.

Fitment and Memorization

Imagine an image of a beach. In the image, there is a white sandy beach accompanied by an ocean that has waves lapping against the shore. Above the horizon in the distance is a clear blue sky, which is somewhat similar in color to the sea. Several seagulls are flying above the water a short distance from the beach. Underfit training could be occurring if the sky is labeled as a body of water in this fictional example. The model concluded that the shade of the sky was similar enough to the images of water in its dataset. Thus, the sky is labeled as water in the output decision. However, overfitting could also cause a model to misclassify an image.

Overfitting gives incorrect conclusions on real-world data as well. Overfitting is like blatant memorization and comes to fruition when a model cannot recognize any new images that are not extremely similar to its training data. To exemplify this, perhaps all the training completed on the overfit model was with images of the sea with boats on the water. When the ML model was trained, it may have evaluated the boats and determined them to be a feature of oceans. To be fair, boats are often found sailing on water, so this is an easy mistake to make. If all the training data fed into a model has boats, an image without a boat may not be classified as being water because the AI application has learned that a body of water must have a boat sailing on its waves to be an ocean, which is a fabricated and inappropriate feature. Algorithms can occasionally recognize features in the noise that are not notable enough to be discovered by a person. Focusing on irrelevant features can ruin a model's ability to generalize to different tasks.

Overfitting is the strict adherence to training data. In short, failing to be able to classify things that belong to a group is overfitting. The purpose of AI and ML is to act in a general way. Creating fake data can sometimes help AI models function better, especially when the data pool is small and more of a certain type is needed. Certain data changes the importance of features because synthetic data appears more frequently. AI that generates images can use those same images as data with the help of its developers. If a computer vision model was made with an appropriate amount of training, some images may have boats while others do not.

Overfit predictions accidentally remain too strict to the data. Scenarios that almost perfectly match the training data can be recognized, while other scenarios dissimilar from the training cannot. Underfit models create both false positives and false negatives because their model is more random and unpredictable in how it handles new data, even though the model may have worked well with the training data. Underfitting is when a machine learning algorithm is ill-suited for real-world use. Creating a formula for a line of best fit that poorly matches data is underfitting. Data can follow patterns, such as curves or other unusual shapes, that are difficult to assign a formula to. Underfitting indicates that the ML model has not witnessed enough data to make good decisions. When a model begins to underfit, both false positives and false negatives (failures to recognize data when there were similarities) can be the result of subpar training. Overfitting and underfitting are pertinent to training, not necessarily the type of failure the outcome produces, although it can provide some evidence as to what is going wrong. Results in output can be chaotic and do not indicate what type of improper fitment happened during training. Either type of poor fitment can cause false positives or false negatives. Overfitting and underfitting can cause failure in the real-world results of an AI model. Optimization refers to a group of techniques in machine learning that helps the model function better in the real world. Optimization helps avoid overfitting and underfitting.

Machine learning helps create algorithms that would otherwise be too expensive to develop. The autonomous nature of ML reduces costs by decreasing development time, and many machine learning models are open-source, meaning they can be shared with anyone interested in using the model. Industry-standard AI models are trained on a network of computers. AI models are expensive and complicated to train, but the model is easy to use by anyone once the application has been developed. Reduction in file size of an AI application is an additional factor that has allowed AI to be tested more easily and used by the public. Some AI computer programs are very small and have been made carefully to limit size to allow installation on devices with limited storage (Wolski, 2023). Programming capabilities that limit the size of applications while increasing their effectiveness is another item on the list of reasons why AI is flourishing in the current decade.

ML uses mathematical formulas to improve its decisions and add layers of depth that complete calculations. A subsequent result of using mathematics to enhance ML is predictive analysis in business. Predictive analysis integrates elaborate calculations to help a business make better financial decisions. ML has become a significant component of making predictions and impactful decisions in business and other fields that supply a significant amount of data. Effectively, businesses rely on a series of choices to navigate the marketplace and continue being profitable. People and businesses that provide services frequently brandish terminology relevant to the field of artificial intelligence, but machine learning techniques improve business leaders' decisions. In any field with extensive data, AI will inherently work and be helpful to people with the knowledge to use the technology.

Deep learning is a subset of machine learning and is named due to its layers of reasoning. Deep learning is a series of checks to manipulate and find patterns in data. Configuring software to check and see if two images are different involves multiple objective questions about the two images, and those checks must be passed to confirm that the images are similar. Deep learning consists of several layers of logic to compare new input data with the algorithms and other processes to create a good result.

Deep learning makes systems more intelligent. To understand deep learning, neural networks must first be understood. A neural network is an interconnected collection of systems, the smallest components of which are nodes. In the biological brain, different parts of the brain handle different functions, although there is communication among those separate sections. Artificial intelligence does not just imitate human processes; human physical attributes are also partially imitated. Treating the brain as a complicated machine and then modeling computer systems and networks after the brain's relative functions is the future of how ANNs will be arranged. The purpose of developing neural networks and DL processes is to enhance AI as a tool that can operate as independently as a person; general artificial intelligence is AI that is roughly as capable as a person. Machines have been designed to help people in the pursuit of living. Neural networks have functioned better in solving problems where a new algorithm was needed. In other words, some tasks are best solved by ML because the most efficient way to complete the task has not yet been discovered, and neural networks have shown promise in being one of the most capable strategies in solving problems that have significant data available.

Machines do not have the same physical and psychological limitations as a person. Humanity will come to discover what a machine's intent could be, even though it must exist in a far different fashion. No complex neural networks have met the requirements of what could be considered a network as intelligent and capable as the brain. The most complicated synthetic neural networks have significant node counts, sometimes ranging into the trillions, but the function of axons in the brain is significantly different than how nodes function in the standard input-output manner AI models use (Nagyfi, 2018). For example, most decision tree nodes are intended to process choices in one direction. Neurons of the brain can create connections to multiple other neurons, and communication can flow in several directions through the neuron. In artificial neural networks, some neurons can flow bidirectionally, but even that format is a newer addition to ML. There is a long way to go before ANNs can fully imitate the human brain's structure, let alone its function. Theoretically, general AI might follow after computer science and neurology convene to create a manmade brain.

Hardware

Lack of computational power limits the capabilities of AI and computer applications in general. The improved capabilities of CPUs and GPUs have allowed AI-related tasks that need tremendous computational power to be effectively computed in a shorter amount of time. Training alone for certain AI applications can take hundreds of hours, and the average cost of training a machine learning model is close to $100 million USD for one lone model. OpenAI has predicted that costs could be closer to $500 million per model by the year 2030 (Yalalov, 2023). Training deep learning models is repetitive, and in most cases, the model completes loops of evaluations. As GPU performance increases, common ML models will increase in performance, as several models rely on GPU capabilities.

Several learning methods exist, but deep learning has been the most effective way of creating an AI system that produces palpable results. Deep learning is an important and powerful aspect of artificial intelligence, but the rate at which AI technologies are currently changing means deep learning could be surpassed. Width and depth are necessities when building the most capable ANNs (Fan et al., 2020). A drawback of deep learning is that it does not use logic to infer how to do something. Multimodal AI (AI that incorporates datasets of different types such as sound, text, and images) will likely cause a system to act more similarly to a human because, like a human, multimodal AI can ingest many types of information. AI behaves more logically when more elaborate information is combined. Multiple modes of data create a context that has a closer semblance to understanding.

AI's historical development has had two notable peaks, and the current development path of AI is raising the apex of progress being made. ML strategies have been introduced in the past that completely changed the field of play. At one time, the concept of backpropagation, which comes from the chain rule in mathematics, allowed for the weight of nodes to be better adjusted in value (Rumelhart et al., 1986). The weight of nodes is how much certain logic layers matter in the context of the task being completed. Rumelhart's work during the 1980s brought significant focus to creating neural networks, changing the direction of AI once again.

AI models can accept multiple types of inputs before arriving at a conclusion. Similarly, when a person thinks about a problem, they consider multiple scenarios. Good problem solvers think about what has happened in the past, the current situation, and what might happen in the future. Taking account of what information is needed and disregarding useless information is as difficult for people as it is for AI. Training and supervising models to function better helps remove bias from the model while adding data with easily identifiable features, resulting in clearer decisions and fewer intermittent errors. AI models with too much training can get confused by non-helpful noise in the data. Later, the chapter "Attentive Listening" will discuss how the model CoAtNet can interpret images of sound and how the model must be trained to ignore noise in images of sound waves.

Some AI applications are developed with numerous servers, while other artificially intelligent applications have a minuscule size and can be stored on a small media storage device like a thumb drive or can be accessed on a website that requires even less CPU power from the user's device. Applications that use deep learning are not developed and subsequently abandoned; models require developers to periodically update the system like a traditional application. After the machine learns and the AI-integrated model is finished being developed just like normal software, it can be left to operate like any other non-AI integrated software, and many models are open source and can be tinkered with via application programming interfaces –a way for anyone to program with less significant strain on a consumer GPU and CPU.

Chapter 2 – The Importance of Datasets in AI

Datasets are extremely important in machine learning. Datasets are like a machine's memories. When pursuing a task, memories are recalled to help complete the task. Algorithms are the engine that drives ML, but the data itself is critical to successful task completion. If ML algorithms are a car, data is the gas. AI cannot work well with bad data. Bad data is a dataset that has poor formatting or is a set of data that is too small or has an overwhelming amount of noise. Datasets may be the most important piece in understanding artificial intelligence because datasets are the memories of an artificially intelligent agent, which will become its conclusive future, particularly in generative AI.

Any data can be made useful with AI, but unlabeled data needs to be labeled before it can be of use. Supervision's main purpose is to label data. When an AI system attempts to predict the weather, the system may replicate weather forecasts from years prior (Dewitte et al., 2021). In some scenarios, an exact replica of a previous forecast may be the initial prediction, which would not be an accurate strategy for predicting the weather but is not a bad point to start at when forecasting. Introducing multiple datasets to be sampled by the machine learning software would greatly enhance a weather forecast and increase the accuracy of the predictions. Having numerous accurate datasets is key to having capable AI systems.

Dimensionality and Making Predictions

Datasets with values capable of being plotted, such as a digital image made of pixels that act as plotted points, have a dimension for each of their plottable points. High dimension is a general term for data sets with more than hundreds of dimensions (Glassner, 2021). Weather data exists for a multitude of places and gives a numerical figure for the high and low-temperature extremes for the day. On The Weather Channel's website, the highs and lows are plotted as points that make up the days of the year. Average temperatures are one part of predicting the weather.

One major advantage of using AI-integrated technology is that it can adapt more than antiquated software. Rapidly changing scenarios are difficult to predict. Weather forecasts are dynamic predictions frequently requiring real-time adjustments to improve past weather forecasts that fit similar conditions. Fortunately for meteorologists, forecasting is greatly improved by data such as records of temperature, precipitation, and wind speed. Using a combination of past techniques and real-time radar predictions is an accurate way to predict weather. Artificial intelligence greatly pales in comparison to human thought, but AI does have a massive advantage in its speed to execute mathematical solutions and the ability to have an exact formula stored that can solve problems. AI implementation is difficult to perfect for applications that face frequently altered situations. Training a system assists AI in completing tasks more effectively, but good datasets are what machine learning models rely on to output information after various algorithms have combined known data to predict an unknown outcome. Scenarios and subjects that have significant amounts of data behind them are perfect platforms for AI to make classifications of the data and provide insight into the future.

Dataset Types

Datasets can be open or closed. Open datasets are referred to in such a way because they are open-source, meaning anyone can access the dataset and utilize it if they are interested in experimenting or making a product. Open-source datasets are hosted on the internet. Closed datasets are proprietary technology and are not shared. Organizations that desire to protect their data often make closed datasets because they do not want to share their technological research with competing companies, or some data can contain personally identifiable information like someone's name which is not ethical to distribute. ML produces outcomes that resemble its dataset. An LLM that samples literature from the nineteenth century will produce text differently than a sampling written during the twenty-first century.

If CV software is tasked with creating images of houses, the software needs to be attached to a dataset with a large quantity (usually thousands or more) of images of homes. The labeled names of the house images are used to affirm to the model what features a typical house would contain.

The way machines handle datasets is typically by way of comparison. Human memories are stored, but memories can be altered with the sprinkling of other new concepts combined with the old. Because of past experiences, new undertakings can be pursued. Experience results in skill at completing tasks. To be creative, a person must be experienced but not mentally repetitive. Broader datasets act as a more experienced mind that can make more reasonable, but not quite rational, decisions. Intelligence that is artificial is not currently able to rationalize circumstances like a person can; AI does not reason. Instead, AI searches for past known circumstances and outcomes to assume future outcomes, while in a supervised system, a human advisor can specify exactly what an outcome is meant to be like.

Datasets of Images

Through the sheer massive volume of example 'memories,' AI will compare images. The images are virtually compared by noting the position of the image's pixels. When two images have similar darker pixels organized in something that looks like the number 5, for example, the software will assume the interpreted image is a 5 if an image is alike enough, which would be evaluated by a percentage when comparing similarity. The likelihood of finding an image that matches a handwritten number increases as the dataset's size increases. Surely, a 5 can be written in only so many ways. One of the most popular open datasets is a massive collection of handwritten digits named the MNIST dataset. The set is comprised of 70,000 total images of numbers 0-9 (LeCun, 1998). The dataset can be utilized to translate an image of written numbers to computer text numbers far faster than a human could transcribe. Many amateur developers exploring machine learning techniques use this basic dataset to experiment. Machine learning is not overly complicated but the computational power of modern computer hardware is like using a sledgehammer to tap a nail into a board.

The handwritten samples are well-organized data for direct use with ML models. Data is not always so well organized. Businesses and organizations retain massive amounts of data.

Cloud and physical storage capabilities have improved so substantially that data stores have exploded in size. Organizations have always strived to maintain and improve operations by relying on past data to make quantitative decisions. Companies have begun using AI programs in customer service, as chatbots that can assist customers. Artificial intelligence's function is contingent on using huge datasets, and improving the means of storing and recalling data will improve AI's capabilities. Data science is one of many scientific fields ingrained in AI research. Where there is a plethora of data, so follows AI. ML applications can be simple and take up a small amount of storage. However, the datasets the application can search through may be incredibly large, such as the CIFAR-10, which contains 60,000 labeled images (Krizhevsky & Hinton, 2009).

An application program interface (API) is a way software can share code between two separate applications. APIs can connect to an external database to attain data so that when a user makes a request, the information will be delivered to the application. When someone goes to look at their credit card balance online, their balance is stored in a database that is not a direct part of the HTML code the website is made from. APIs make applications more complicated and insecure when improperly configured. However, they also allow data to be shared among different applications, and with data sharing comes new insights on all manner of things.

An Abundance of Data

Narrow artificial intelligence is what all current applications of artificially intelligent systems accomplish. With the current state of technology, AI-integrated systems are intended to solve certain problems under specific conditions. The system then needs substantial handholding (by a human) to accomplish the task. No platforms exist that show artificial general intelligence because no platforms can perform tasks almost identical to how an individual would reason and look to implement solutions with creativity, broad awareness, and past experiences. Artificially intelligent systems have an ever-broadening range of resources to utilize, however. The internet is host to an enormous amount of stuff that increases daily. The internet is projected to grow to 175 zetabytes by 2025 (Rydning et al., 2018). A huge store of information grows along with the internet. Current estimates predict the internet doubles in domain names (websites) you can visit every 5.32 years (Zhang et al., 2008). The publicly hosted sources of information the internet provides are greatly beneficial to enhancing artificial and human intelligence alike.

With the advent of the internet, an event called an information explosion occurred. An information explosion results from data and information rapidly multiplying, a term that means humanity's ability to retain a collection of information that is growing exponentially larger. The storage and abundant means of retrieval the internet provides for information is unprecedented. With humanity's growing cornucopia of data, AI systems will continue to flourish. Data accessibility is becoming more prevalent, catering to use cases for people and software alike.

Web Crawling and Web Scraping

A nonprofit organization was formed in 2008 that began crawling the web. The organization is named Common Crawl. A quote from Common Crawl's website states, "Open Data fosters interdisciplinary collaborations that can drive greater efficiency and effectiveness in solving complex challenges, from environmental issues to public health crises. Overall, embracing Open Data from web crawls enriches society with innovation, empowerment, and collaboration." (Crawl, 2024). The organization's statements suggest how datasets have impactful effects on making societal progress using data. The internet is such a virtualized deep abyss that organizing the data hosted online is tremendously complicated. Common Crawl has completed substantial groundwork to allow artificial intelligence models to access organized data, which helps in task completion. People also have direct access to this data. The mission of this nonprofit is to store and distribute datasets for all who want to use them. Amazon Web Services hosts Common Crawl's data via their cloud services. Large corporations, such as Microsoft, have their own datasets that developers can use, but Common Crawl is not anchored to a business and does not support any business's commercial interests.

Internet Archive is a website that hosts billions of books, videos, audio, and software. Internet Archive's "digital library" grows larger every day (Archive, 2024). Internet Archive is a rare resource, and because a non-profit group maintains the website, nothing hosted by the site is for sale. Internet-hosted repositories of information are very important because data is frequently destroyed. Web scraping and web crawling are methods of saving information on a website or other source available online. For example, a website that shows a list of their employees, along with contact information, can be saved to a file by web crawlers. LLMs like Bert and Chat GPT leverage Common Crawl because it downloads Wikipedia articles used for general information. Many free-to-use web scrapers exist, such as Octoparse and Beautiful Soup. These applications are not simple to use, but they are very powerful tools that retrieve data from the internet. AI uses different tools to attain data from websites. In most cases, the data will need to be formatted so the AI system can use the data in a labeled format.

Mathematics is home to numerous algorithms that can help datasets improve ML's ability to complete tasks. Despite AI's recent practical success, several of the mathematical algorithms involved in AI have been used for hundreds of years. Most theories of mathematics are complex, but when applied to ML, simple functions can have a massive effect.

Chapter 3 – Mathematics and Probability in AI

Mathematical integration into ML is far more interesting than mathematics on its own. A basic understanding of mathematics is necessary to understand AI. Mean is the average of a collection of numbers. Median is the number positioned in the middle of a list of numbers. Mode is a value that appears the most frequently among a list of numbers. These three things may appear to be simple, but together, they are extremely significant in enabling machines to learn features in data.

Optimization

Global optimization is a complex term for a maximum or minimum point in a graphed mathematical function. The maximum and minimum points in data help provide evidence of what data is normal and what data are outliers. The importance of this mathematical concept to AI is that output data is intended to be like the dataset, meaning a normal benchmark needs to be taken from the dataset.

An imaginary AI model could be tasked with making music. The goal of this hypothetical system is to make the perfect elevator music. The music must be slow, naturally staving off the intrinsic terror of riding in an elevator. The developers of the music-making system need to create a model that will learn from data, so a collection of one hundred of the finest songs from the (definitely real) elevator music genre is assembled. When the model evaluates the songs, algorithms that evaluate tempo determine the data sample's beats per minute (BPM). Creating a function to determine the average

BPM is simple and will insert a node of mathematical logic into the model, which is good because the average helps to quantify what the model will produce. The next node will evaluate the dataset's global maximum and minimum BPM. The songs created by the model will unnerve the elevator passengers if they are too fast, but if the songs are too slow, they will barely sound like music. Determining useful features (patterns) of the one hundred sample songs will help create a song that adheres to the genre.

Bootstrapping is a method to create a sample of a population. If workers at an aquarium needed to evaluate the fish in an aquarium to find the most common type of fish, they could bootstrap a population of thousands of fish to uncover which are the most abundant. The bootstrapped results can make it easy to find ratios in the aquarium, such as the ratio of sharks to manta rays. Bootstrapping is especially useful when you have a large group of things that need a summarized description. Feature determination shares similarities with bootstrapping in creating insights that help ML learn about data. A population that has been bootstrapped displays ratios, such as the theoretical ratio of sharks to manta rays, in the aquarium.

The Mathematics of Lines

Linear algebra is used extensively throughout many machine learning models. Linear algebra, describing the field most simply, is the mathematical study of lines. Understanding lines can help predict outcomes. Making accurate predictions, i.e., probability, is pivotal to AI's success at completing tasks.

Without linear algebra, artificial intelligence would not be possible. Linear regression is a popular algorithm that can model future outcomes and is easy to implement with basic code. Regression tasks in ML are used to predict outcomes that occur along a linear basis. Linear regression shows the trend of points on a graph. If the points begin to cluster upwards, so will the linear regression model. Plotted points on a graph immediately reveal trends, like upward or downward trending, in the data.

After taking in a substantial amount of input data, a machine learning model will frequently create a formula that models a line of best fit. Linear algebra is used by ML algorithms to create equations that effectively summarize large portions of data. The equation that is created from the data will then be used to predict the y output of x variables. CV uses algebraic matrices to rotate the edge lines made from dataset images to see if they match up with tested images.

Playing a game of basketball requires a player to understand that shooting farther from the hoop is less likely to score than closer shot attempts. The basketball player's mind does not give an exact figure of how likely it is, but there is a point where a shooter loses reasonable confidence in making a basket because they are too far from the hoop to be accurate. Probability partially affects how professional athletes play, but for computers, probability is the majority of how a decision is computed in AI. Probability is the best way to gain practical confidence when completing a task. Machine learning applications can compute probabilities of different outcomes much faster than people. A basketball player does not have time to bring out a TI-84 calculator, a piece of paper, a pencil, and an abacus while on the court. They have other ways of knowing their chances of making a basket at different ranges and positions.

Thomas Bayes' Theorems

Many effective AI algorithms exist that do not involve neural networks. Neural networking is an excellent showcase of the advanced state of technology computer science and mathematics have produced, but simplicity is effective and palpable in AI. Storage limitations, especially on smartphones and devices with limited storage, require ingenuity in creating smaller AI systems. Reverend Thomas Bayes contributed significant concepts of combining probability during the middle of the 18th century that are still used today. Bayes (1763) presented methods for formulating a probability that relied on another probability's likelihood. Bayesian ideologies are subsequently a way of showing estimated predictions. Bayesian probabilities are written as a range of percentages, such as 10%-35%, due to the non-exact nature of combining probabilities. Bayes' theorems are an example of how ML algorithms can operate outside of human psychology. People can hamper decision-making and contribute to bias; mathematics helps sanitize ML's decisions of mistakes. Simple decision trees can be heavy-handed when it comes to making guesses, and a good guess is all that some people request from AI. Useful predictions exist, but none are exact within the Bayesian method of estimation.

Conditional probability is the likelihood that something will happen due to something else occurring. Staying consistent with sports, in baseball, probabilities are handed out freely to quantify nearly every metric imaginable. Pitchers have statistics on how often they throw pitches that are hit out of the park for a home run. Batters also have numerous statistics, one of which is a value that predicts how likely it is that the batter will hit a home run. The statistics from the pitcher and batter combine to give a range of probabilities for what may happen during the batter's turn at the plate. The sport of baseball takes place as probabilities are brought to reality in the field of play.

Bayesian modeling pertains to two events, referred to as A and B, representing the events. Four scenarios are pertinent to using the Bayesian model to make a prediction: What is the probability of A happening? What is the probability of B happening? If A happens, how likely is B to occur? Conversely, if B occurs, how likely is A? Combining estimates allows for elaborate scenarios to be quantifiably predicted.

Out of the Ordinary

Anomaly detection in cybersecurity uses probability models to discover irregular activities that have occurred despite being statistically unlikely. Antivirus software fights malware by taking snapshots of normal system processes and alarming when those processes deviate in processing demands or new processes suddenly appear. Organizations with networks that contain business-related data must keep their digital infrastructure secure. To understand normal activity on a network or host device, ML needs to take place to recognize normal events that happen daily and usually at the same time. A significant uptick in network traffic will likely be witnessed at 9 a.m. on nearly any involved with a business. Traffic is generated by employees and customers visiting websites in the business's domain and employees logging into their computers via active directory. High amounts of traffic are possibly normal during business hours. However, a network anomaly detection system will likely create an alert for traffic peaking at a twenty-four-hour high at 3 am. Any number of issues could be present, from an attack to a misconfiguration, all of which are noted by anomaly detection via ML recognizing inconsistencies in activity.

Visualizations of Math

Different mathematical equations and formulas are needed to meet the diverse requirements of AI models. Gradient descent is a way to optimize and predict outcomes that work well with large datasets. Unsupervised machine learning can quickly take vast amounts of disorganized data and display that in a simple, useful format. Manifold learning becomes pertinent when a value prediction is impossible to make through any linear means. Another name for manifold learning is nonlinear dimensionality reduction, a name that rolls right off the tongue. A manifold is a representation of high-dimensional data in a format that is plotted onto a graph. Manifolds simplify complex information. The manifold most people think of is the exhaust piece on a car's engine. The manifold has multiple chambers that are reduced into one that extends to the tailpipe, thus reducing the metal tubes into one chamber.

When looking at a satellite image of the continent of Africa on Google Earth, features of the continent, like the Sahara Desert and the dark green patches that make up the forests of Central Africa, are highly visible. When these two geological features are represented on a map, they are displayed like a manifold. Satellite images can be very high quality under the right conditions. Rather than the specific vibrant colors satellite imagery provides, the Sahara Desert is tan colored, and jungles are simply green in maps that have been manifolded. Maps are far from being photo-real, yet they frequently contain more information in a less cluttered way. More information is better than less, but more noise makes it harder to see geographic landmarks on a map. Manifolds lower the dimensionality of displayed data. A manifold is a local perspective of a broader shape in the case of most maps. Sometimes, the object being manifolded is represented in a spectrum of colors that have been reduced to simpler pixels, such as taking a high-resolution photo and making the image appear grainier, like a printed comic illustration.

Artificial intelligence can have difficulties operating in a general fashion. Functioning in the real world, instead of training environments, requires appropriate ML algorithms. Anscombe's quartet is when four commonalities (like mean, median, mode, or range) exist in two datasets, even though the graphed points are not similar. Anscombe's theories display how machine learning algorithms can make mistakes, even when there is a significant amount of data. In plotting x and y coordinates, numerous similarities can be found in correlation, variance, average, and line of best fit. The mathematician Alberto Cairo (2016) has made an example that plots data into images shaped like an X, a star, a dinosaur, and nine other images to make up the Datasaurus Dozen to showcase how data can appear to be incidentally related. The graphs show completely different images all with the same statistics. Means, medians, and modes being related do not necessarily affirm that data is similar. However, pseudo-consistent data can cause AI to find patterns that are not relevant. Data should be graphed to see its visual attributes.

Computers are effective at completing brute-force calculations. Typing 5! into a calculator immediately results in the solution. ! is a factorial. The way factorials are solved for this equation is 5 x 4 x 3 x 2 x 1, which equals 120. Calculating factorials using pencil and paper is tedious, yet a calculator can accomplish such a task in a fraction of a second. Humanity has employed computers to help make calculations, subsequently helping people make better decisions. Computers work well for this purpose because they can do brute-force calculations extremely fast, but computers can also be creative. The creativity machines can produce is purely coincidental but nonetheless effective. The precise nature of using mathematics to make decisions can also produce results different than most human decision-making.

AI applications use different machine learning models at different levels. More complicated models integrate more layers of complex logic into the application, which can create developmental and operational challenges. Specific examples of AI models address tasks or problems, such as CV and language processing.

Chapter 4 – Artificial Intelligence Models

There are different types of models in artificial intelligence. The variation in models is a result of what the model is used for. Computer vision is the evaluation of images and video to classify aspects of the media. In the field of deep learning, ResNet and YOLO (You Only Look Once) are models that cater to computer vision.

A group of Microsoft researchers wanted to develop an AI model that required fewer resources but would still be capable of evaluating hundreds of layers of logic. The model developed by the team had 152 layers, resulting in one version of the residual network being named ResNet-152 (He et al., 2016). Evaluating such a significant number of layers takes time, even when a small number of features are being searched for in the dataset. ResNet models contain mathematical equations and other types of layers weighted by the significance of their impacts on the outcome of data flowing through ResNet, thus changing how computations flow and saving time. A model with more layers is generally more accurate and makes more nuanced decisions as each layer refines the outcome of things input into the model. ResNet uses skip connections, which significantly reduces computation time; during the process of residual networking, every step that is not needed will be skipped. Not all AI models are capable of skipping unneeded layers of logic. The dichotomy of residual networks is that what a model does is important, but what a model does not do is just as critical. Computer scientists are working on the broad pursuit of making AI more cognitively capable; understanding dichotomies is a necessity for achieving balance in logical decision-making. Good decisions do not result from binary yes or no logic. As an example, if an image were going to be produced by a generative CV program, a black-and-white image would allow numerous layers to be skipped over because the model would primarily deal with creating edge lines and not have to be concerned with knowing where colors go, other than black and white. The ordered roll call style process ML goes through is not exceptionally intuitive. Residual networking saves time.

CV

Both ResNet and YOLO can be configured and trained to recognize objects in images. Objects recognized by computer vision programs frequently outline the object with a square that includes a text label that denotes the object's name. The impact of being able to evaluate the frames of a video quickly is important in many applications, especially in autonomous vehicles. The camera systems in self-driving automobiles need to be able to rapidly identify objects that are near the car. When an autonomous vehicle is driving down the road, driving over a small stick is much less significant than driving over a piece of metal that happens to closely resemble a stick. Sticks do not fall far from the metaphorical decision tree. Being able to identify objects in video or images is a critical skill of machines that need to navigate independently. Autonomous cars and robots, not to mention other machine vision contraptions that work on assembly lines, will need to have cameras that can record at very high resolutions and be able to discern what different objects are near the machine. CV indicates an AI application that manipulates or creates images, while machine vision is a use of CV to directly enhance a machine most often in an industrial setting. Cameras have greatly improved in their ability to record in high resolutions and high refresh rates in the last two decades, and many cameras are small enough to be easily attached to a vehicle. Higher-resolution images have more clearly defined edges that comprise the perimeters of shapes in an image. Another way of describing edges is color boundaries. A blurry image looks the same to a machine as to a person. Blurriness is a lack of strict borders in color in an image. To have the best detection of objects in an image, high resolution is helpful but not mandatory. New strategies are being produced daily that are helping to find edges in images that are low resolution (Polansky et al., 2024).

One popular AI model that is publicly available to anyone on the internet is Stable Diffusion. Stable Diffusion creates images that have been prompted by text typed by a user. A person can type in specific words to the textbox, and the model will produce an image that correlates with the prompt. Stable Diffusion is different from other diffusion-based AI models because it can be run on a standard graphics processing unit, meaning most all personal computers could run Stable Diffusion (Face, 2023). The dataset stable diffusion uses is called LAION 5B The list is a staggering five billion images, all with image tags that describe the image. Tags attached to the images in LAION-5B assist Stable Diffusion in working towards an outcome. A simple prompt that says "chicken in a field" frequently results in the output image containing both a chicken and a field, with some images looking slightly odd. All the images that happen to be of chickens and fields are labeled as such within the dataset, and Stable Diffusion's final product is an amalgamation of those two things.

After a prompt has been sent to Stable Diffusion, the model begins by making an image that looks like colorful noise, all of which happens on the backend and is not visible to the user until the final picture is finished. There are forty steps in Stable Diffusion's process, and with each step, the image gets more clearly defined, and distinguishable features take shape. The image goes from sparks of color that look like television static to discernible splotches of blurry color to a high-definition image, depending on the dataset used. Stable Diffusion uses a U-Net block, which is a way to structure encoders and their respective decoders. Stable Diffusion is built with ResNet as its base model (Alammar, 2022).

ResNet can also label images with text descriptions of the objects that appear in the images, reversing the process of prompted image creation. For people who are blind, text descriptions of images increase their accessibility to information. The archaic term "moving pictures" alludes to how AI could transcribe films or videos into text descriptions with modifications to the base ResNet model. AI applications can help improve the accessibility of information in all formats.

Similar to how machine learning classifies features of a dataset, AI is very good at making summaries of information using large language models. Suppose a theoretical AI network could "watch" a film. After the viewing, information about the film could be rapidly stored. A film is made up of two major components: images and audio. However, films have subtitles that act as a transcript and some even have audio descriptions of what is happening on screen. Multimodal AI combines different types of systems like CV and LLMs together to become capable of ingesting datasets that contain different types of data like images and text. A multimodal AI system that leverages computer vision and a large language model could classify a film's images, audio, and subtitles to organize the data into numerous useful things very quickly. One of those useful things could be a description of the movie that could write the plot's narrative while separating character conversations into quoted sections, just like a novel. Reflexively, a multimodal system that combines CV and language modeling capabilities can theoretically convert a book into a film by creating visualizations from the text and audio from quoted passages.

Search Engines

Google Search has AI technologies incorporated into how it functions. The way that search results are presented to a user is different for everyone. Recommendations will appear when using Google's new search engine feature that is currently being tested (Reid, 2023). When developing its search engine, Google used machine learning techniques to find more accurate search results. Another incorporation of AI that the search engine uses is CV. The ability to search for images using text is common, and millions of people search for images daily. However, another way of searching exists called Google Lens. Rather than typing text into the search box with the intent to find images, Lens will accept an image file (or link to an image) and then search using the selected image as searchable criteria. Lens will respond by showing a large group of images with similar visual features to the searched image. Microsoft has a similar technology called Bing Visual Search.

Many aspects of an image can be evaluated for features. An incredibly important feature of images is the edge lines around the perimeter of different objects in an image. Removing highly detailed aspects of an image and just using the general edges is a basic requirement for CV to evaluate an image. CV applications have labeled datasets so the system knows what certain objects are by their labels. However, the task of the application is to find features of an image which then remain associated with the label. A common application of CV is to recognize the human face. If a person's face is broken down into edges, the shape of their head and the outline of their eyes, nose, and mouth become visible. Once the edges are created, a dataset containing images with perimetric edges can be referenced to compare images. The evaluated image acts as a filter and is placed on top of numerous images to create a contrast between both images' lines. The images are compared by how close the edges are to one another. If the edges are similar enough (a certain percentage of likeness needs to be met), the image is determined to contain a person's face.

Shooting the Breeze

Despite AI's lesser-known implementation into numerous commonly used applications, like Spotify and Facebook, Chat GPT is one of the most widely known direct experiences anyone can have with AI. Users directly conversate with chatbots, which exemplifies many of Turing's ideas on how biological intelligence (humans) communicate with artificial intelligence. Spotify and Facebook's web-based applications are not immediately recognizable as being integrated with AI. The backend of these applications enhances user experiences on their respective applications and creates a unique experience for the user by developing ideas of what certain types of users want to see or hear.

Chat GPT (a product of Open AI) gained significant acclaim after its introduction on November 30, 2022 (Schulman, 2022). Since the inception of Chat GPT-3, the LLM has become one of the most popular chatbots, and in January 2023, the application had 100 million users, making it the most rapidly used piece of software in history (Hu, 2023). The multimodal Chat GPT-4 has progressed to the point of being able to write several types of documents successfully combined with CV capabilities. Writing a PowerPoint or instructions for simple tasks can easily be achieved with Chat GPT. Language models can have issues with accuracy because of how they predict sentences. LLMs are frequently called chatbots, although some language models are intended for purposes other than chatting, like translating languages or organizing large collections of texts. The most common interaction with an LLM is to ask the program questions. The LLM will then respond with what it predicts to be the best answer. Not all answers are accurate because creating responses by committee, so to speak, is not how to communicate properly. The term hallucinations is used to describe how chatbots accidentally produce inaccurate results. LLMs can accidentally produce nonsensical outputs because as the chatbot formulates a statement, prior words in the sentence predict the next word to be placed in order, resulting in a hallucinated word being slotted into a certain place in a sentence because the LLM expects a related word to follow certain words, which is not always appropriate.

Numerous problems currently exist with all LLMs, but one of the most predominant is that there is no way of explaining how a language model acquired a specific response. Since ChatGPT frequently combines answers from datasets where a limited amount of data is used (likely because a limited amount of data exists), the language model can produce biased and inaccurate responses from the lack of information. However, ChatGPT and other language models, such as BERT, are improving rapidly because of text library databases that can be easily accessed online. Common Crawl has greatly improved ChatGPT's capabilities. Common Crawl sorts through billions of web pages, and those pages are archived in the dataset.

Google's LLM BERT has progressed rapidly in its effective use in natural language translation. Bidirectional Encoder Representations from Transformers (BERT) is Google's system of language modeling (Devlin et al., 2018). Natural language processing tasks, such as complex language translations, have been accomplished more easily by way of transformers being used in one of their most effective forms. The rather gruffly named BERT was trained on Wikipedia and the BookCorpus, a conglomeration of 7,000 books from the independent book platform Smashwords (Bandy & Vincent, 2021). The ability of BERT to do extremely well in formal natural language understanding tests likely stems from its ability to use self-attention to find context for a word. The 'Bidirectional' component this LLM uses allows it to check the word before and after a specific word. In the sentence "The fast car sped away.," the words beside car are fast and sped. BERT does not comprehend why certain words would be used, but the model can discern when a certain word commonly appears between two others. Fortunately, nouns are frequently accompanied by certain verbs and adjectives in English, allowing BERT to use words that match the tone of a text when completing translations. Google Search uses BERT to improve its search results by relating different but similar searches to one another.

PaLM 2, Pathways Language Model, also developed by Google, is an LLM that was created to handle more general tasks and has an interface similar to a chatbot. PaLM can complete tasks in math and can also write code. Further development by Google's DeepMind and Brain teams has led to Gemini, which combines text-based and image AI into one multimodal model (McIntosh et al., 2023). Gemini is the most advanced system Google has developed and can use different types of data inputs to learn, such is the way with multimodal AI. Gemini has garnered massive media coverage, but the model is too new to be well-researched and tested, so its capabilities will be uncovered over time.

AI and Hacking

Simple attacks such as buffer overflows have affected various language models. With buffer overflows, symbols, and text that are intended to query a database can result in the chatbot functioning poorly or not as intended. A group of Google researchers discovered that certain text input into Chat GPT's prompt resulted in the model directly relaying information from its training data (Nasr et al., 2023). Chatbots always have a textbox where a user can type things to interact with the system. These text boxes need to be protected from attack, just as any program that allows text entry should. Certain lines of code can be input that can directly show items from the model's database or other information that is not intended to be released by the chatbot. Chat GPT is not an open-source system. LLMs are intended to create unique responses; at no point are chatbots supposed to output information from a dataset in its original form. LLM systems use databases to query data, meaning other attacks that work against databases may also be functional attack vectors for LLMs that have publicly accessible text boxes. The extremely cutting-edge nature of AI applications sometimes pushes systems into production when they are not ready for public use. Financial interests often cause software updates to be released prematurely. If developers do not troubleshoot, hackers will troubleshoot for them, with far more devastating consequences. All public-facing web applications can be attacked, which is typically discovered after an incident. AI is not immune to illicit vulnerabilities that all software shares. Developers should be cautious when making software that can be used by the general public.

Art Intertwined

Text and images are frequently manipulated by AI, but AI also has the capability to change and create audio. Using music as an example, a computer program could be designed to determine the volume, frequency range, and beats per minute of a song. Each aspect determined is a deeper layer. The software can then attempt to make a song that follows the user's specified guidelines. Currently, this example does not work flawlessly. Musical AI applications can provide unexpected or improper results. When the utility makes songs, there are usually no distinct instruments. This makes the music sound unusual and vague. Sometimes, there are distinct parts of the song that come close to being similar to human-made music, but the music is always peculiar sounding or even boring and too simple. More than likely, AI sound models will develop well enough to make good music, but for now, sounds meant to please people are best made by themselves. Music is art, and AI does not always hit its mark when developing complex art meant for human enjoyment.

The arts are colliding in the world of AI, which was predictable because all media regarding the human experience are congruently intertwined. Multimodal AI will capitalize on these interconnections. Language, images, and sound define how humans interact with each other, whether in the form of art or more simple communication. In the pursuit of artificial intelligence, language models and computer vision are finding successful ways to have computers engage in media. Artificial intelligence is allowing the plethora of manmade art to be put to good use, not just for the betterment of people but also for the enhancement of machine's capabilities.

Deep learning models are becoming the mainstay of machine learning due to the success of deeply layered models like DALL-E 3, Stable Diffusion, and Chat GPT-4, which have become successful functionally and financially. DALL-E is a CV application that creates images from text prompts. Both Chat GPT and DALL-E are available for the general public to use on OpenAI's website. Stable Diffusion is also accessible online but is more commonly used via an API. Stable Diffusion's API is a way of writing programs that use Stable Diffusion without having to have powerful hardware to physically run the program. Stability (the creator of this model) provides the hardware resources that the generative

AI relies on. Resources are accessed by an internet connection from a computer application to Stable Diffusion's model.

Writing Code

Anyone can start writing code that leverages ML algorithms or entire AI models. Many coding languages, such as Python and Julia, can be used for machine learning and mathematics modeling. Today, making AI applications is easier than ever. Where ease begins, so ends struggle, and thus follows abundance. Linear algebra has existed in programming since the inception of modern programming languages in the 1990s. Programming languages and toolkits that cater to probability and numerical analysis provide the capability to develop tasks for ML. As mentioned, AI applications rely on datasets, and programming an AI application often requires the new application to be connected to a dataset. Open-source AI models can be reattached to different datasets to get different results. Julia is a language that has made substantial progress in computational learning and AI. CV and robotics tasks have been developed using code written in programming languages like Julia.

Code libraries that help developers write code with ML integration are becoming more common. Meta's development team has released PyTorch. PyTorch consists of various pre-built code frameworks to begin natural language modeling and image object identification. The Linux Foundation hosts and now maintains the open-source repositories for PyTorch's code under its own name: PyTorch Foundation. Tesla Autopilot, Tesla's self-driving automobile technology, was built with PyTorch. The broad-reaching Linux community has also completed substantial work to enable AI to reach the state it currently exists in. Code banks enable developers to access AI model Apis much more easily. Without code banks, students and researchers would not have the necessary resources to build AI applications. Businesses would also suffer from a lack of open-source maintenance and distribution. Easier access to code progresses the field of computer programming by enabling anyone to learn about application development.

Encoding, Decoding, and Transforming

Transformers are making a key difference in progressing neural networks. A group of researchers completed experiments in language translation tasks, which has implications for other systems that use encoders and decoders when text in a language is translated into a different language. The researchers discovered that rather than using convolutions and recurrence, a transformer could be used instead (Vaswani et al., 2017). Transformers are used in language translation to accurately manipulate sentences from one language into another by focusing on significant parts of the sentence, like verbs or adjectives. Language translation tasks are challenging to perform because words cannot always be directly translated with both languages being perfectly parallel. In other words, differing grammar rules can cause words to not be in a one-to-one order in different languages. Because of the alternate design of transformers and its impacts on the model, less training time is needed when using transformers, to some extent deprecating convolutional and recurrent networks. The unique attribute of transformers is how they handle large quantities of input data. When an artificial intelligence model evaluates input data, a finite number of features can be noted, and the more input information there is, the more detail is lost. However, transformers can help prevent some of this loss.

Chapter 5 – Attentive Listening

Pressing different keys on a keyboard makes different sounds; some people (and many house cats) enjoy the clattering sound of typing. Many typists can recognize a few specific sounds a keyboard makes, such as the irregular clack of the spacebar and the sudden tapping of the backspace key when a mistake is made. However, a person is not capable of discerning what someone is typing by simply listening because keypresses sound too similar. The variations in the sound profile of the "k" key are nearly the same as the "x" key in the human ear, even though they are slightly different. Several studies have researched how to record the sounds of a person typing and then translate the racket of typing into the actual recorded keypresses.

Side Channel Attacks in Cybersecurity

Side channel attacks (SCAs) are techniques that can be used to analyze a computer to exploit the machine or discover information about the device's use that would otherwise be hidden or protected. Side channel attacks consistently involve using power draw monitoring, electromagnetic leaks, and sounds that result from using a device. Any release of observable data, such as sounds or electronic frequencies, is what SCAs attempt to leverage. Most modern PCs and laptops use solid-state drives, which do not have any moving parts. Hard disc drives (HDD) have a disc that can be written to and read from in the device, and the disc spins as a part of normal operation. HDDs make noise and begin to vibrate—a ramping up noise—when starting a program or doing something else that prompts the drive to begin reading or writing on the disk. CPU usage increases the heat of the CPU's cores and causes fans in a PC to spin faster. Hard drives increasing in revolutions per minute or fans increasing in speed are two releases of information that allude to the computer's activity. Both are unintended and are potential frameworks for attack. Simply by listening or feeling a device, a person may be able to recognize that the CPU (central processing unit) or HDD is completing computations at a higher rate as vibrations become more intense.

Subtleties of Sound

Exploiting the regular use of a computer is what side-channeling is all about. Computers emit different frequencies. Some of the frequencies are easily noted, such as the light emitted from the monitor or sounds from speakers or headphones. Other frequencies, such as the 2.4 gigahertz electromagnetic waves Bluetooth communicates with, are not possible for a human to hear or see. Some side-channel attacks involve intercepting Bluetooth waves from a wireless keyboard and translating them into keyboard presses. However, if an attacker could be within audible range of the sounds of typing to stage an attack, that would be a much easier attack to implement and require less advanced hardware than monitoring electromagnetic leaks.

On August 3, 2023, three people from various UK universities published their findings on using an audio side channel attack to snoop on a test subject typing. The research that Joshua Harrison, Ehsan Toreini, and Maryam Mehrnezhad completed has helped bring attention to side-channel attacks and ML-based hacking. As a result of machine learning becoming more effective at comparing massive quantities of data, SCAs are becoming more common. SCAs and other types of hacking are manipulating PCs and smartphones in new ways due to ML's enhanced capabilities.

The deep learning techniques used by the group have surpassed previous attempts to record keyboard usage to reveal what a person is typing. The team managed to accurately predict 95% of the keystrokes, which is more than enough to comprehend the gist of a typed conversation. The team pursued a second scenario, which was set up to record the keystrokes via Zoom. Zoom uses noise reduction algorithms that make sound frequencies harder to evaluate due to a loss in quality. Despite the lower-quality audio recordings, 93% accuracy was achieved with Zoom (Harrison et al., 2023). Being able to use a video conferencing application allows for remote recording of keystrokes, expanding landscapes of attack.

The device targeted by the researcher's experiments was a MacBook Pro from 2021. MacBook Pros are common laptops, and due to the similar nature in which Mac designs their keyboards, other Mac laptops could theoretically be recorded and analyzed with similar results. The fact that there are only so many keyboards, key switches, and key membranes makes acquiring a large dataset of keystroke noises significantly easier. An iPhone recorded the sounds emanating from the keyboard as a person typed. iPhones contains a microphone at the bottom and another at the top of the device.

The deep learning model that was used is called CoAtNet, which has a record of producing industry-standard evaluations of images. Google's Brain team created CoAtNet. The parameters of CoAtNet are made of two convolutional layers of depth and then two global layers (Dai et al., 2021). Deep learning always has more than three layers, but the structure of different models can vary. CoAtNet is a shortened version of the phrase convolution and attention networks. The convolutional layer is the first layer in a network. Convolutions are snapshots of a portion of a larger grid. When a convolution operation takes place, the operation summarizes a grid in a fashion somewhat similar to how mathematical manifolds are made. In the form of image analysis (which is CoAtNet's forte), small sections of an image are convoluted into a newly partitioned grid. The new grid will have identifiers to show the section's related features. An image editing software blurs and sharpens images by using convolutions through a similar method. The range of different pixel color values is combined to make an average color, which results in blurring. Since CoAtNets is being used as a CV application (the audio is in the form of images of soundwaves) the purpose of the convolutional layer is to turn the images into what is effectively a graph of numbers the model can better understand and organize.

SCAs against keyboards benefit from being close to the accurate key, even when the guess made was not the right key. The model used by Harrison and others did not account for distances; CoAtNet only compared images to determine which key was pressed. Implementing a system of approximating which key was pressed on location could have made the CoAtNet model even more accurate but immensely more complicated to create. This experiment also did not use a language model, which would have acted like a spell-checker to make more accurate predictions. Considering the hardware used in this experiment primarily consisted of a fake victim's laptop and an iPhone to record keyboard sounds, the results are incredible. The real muscle behind SCAs is machine learning's ability to organize data.

The team practicing this technique used mel-spectrogram images to compare the sounds of keystrokes. Traditional soundwave visualizations were not as effective as a spectrogram in showing the frequencies a keystroke sound is made of. Spectrograms contain more visual information than a traditional waveform representation of sound. A spectrogram is created by using a sound and splitting the sample into multiple frames that are combined to produce the image of a noise over time. CoAtNet needs as much detail as possible when comparing the images of the spectrograms.

Both a human and CoAtNet can notice how spectrograms of keyboard sounds look different, and the subtle differences are massively important in finding the correct key. The CoAtNet attention layer follows the convolutional layer and determines what characteristics are most important. If CoAtNet was configured to recognize Dalmatians, an attention layer that requires the network to be able to ensure a dog is black and white before proceeding onto other layers of logic to make further evaluations is an example of the type of prerequisite parameters attention uses. Convolutional layers may sound complicated, but in this case, the convolution is the first layer of logic that evaluates an image. A convolutional layer places a filter over an image to find patterns in the image. During supervised training of the system, filters document variances in images. The spectrograms that the CoAtNet model analyzed could have numerous attributes. If enough attributes of the image look the same as a dataset image, the system will know a certain key was typed.

One example of a similar experimental attack recorded the presses on a virtualized keyboard on a smartwatch and smartphone. Typing on a smartphone (or smartwatch) causes the device to move very slightly, which is recorded by the device's positioning sensors. The incidental device movements typing causes are similar enough that ML can recognize positional changes in the phone as typed words. Naturally, typing on a phone causes the device to tilt and lean slightly as both thumbs are pressed against the screen. Smartwatches move similarly. Gyroscopes, accelerometers, and a technology that records the plotted coordinates of screen touches all contributed to determining what a user was typing (Maiti et al., 2018).

One threat model constructed allowed for an 83% accuracy in determining what was typed into the phone's virtual keyboard (Lin & Seibel, 2019). These are impressive results when considering that the technology used in the experimental attack is intended for use, such as with GPS (global positioning system) navigation and not to record minuscule accidental movements made on the device when typing.

The scientists completing the aforementioned experiments are world-class ML experts, and staging an attack with SCAs that use sound frequencies or GPS sensors is not something a person who is not an expert in the field could easily accomplish. Dozens of researchers have spent years working towards using various forms of AI to stage experimental attacks. To say the least, SCAs leveraging ML are not currently seen in the wild, but the researchers did an excellent job in continuing to progress on prior research, and their actions revealed potential threats SCAs could pose when assisted by AI.

Two factors will increase the prevalence of ML-based side-channel attacks. The first is that keyboard keys are actually caps. The mechanism that registers the keypress is a toggle-style button underneath the cap called a switch. There are mechanical switches, and there are membranous switches. However, not very many mechanical and membrane switches exist. Furthermore, there are only dozens of popular keyboard designs, and most designs are pretty similar. With such a small number of different switches and keyboards, most keyboards will sound very similar when typed upon, and that means a good-quality dataset of keystroke sounds would not be too noisy (no pun intended). The limited number of available switches and keyboard models make SCA attacks much more effective and easier to implement.

Paying Close Attention

Self-attention, in terms of neural networking, helps to make better decisions with more data. For example, an artificially intelligent system might be trying to assume what word a collection of recorded keystrokes is. The word typed was "quietly," but the software translated the keyboard sounds into "quieyly." The "y" in that word is an error, which the system can discover through self-attention because the other six letters in the word and their positions make the word most likely to be "quietly." Funnily enough, when AI makes a wrong guess, it can appear very similar to how a human mistypes a key: the key is near to what both parties intended the key press to be. AI making a close initial guess is valuable when a person reads the results and determines what key was really pressed.

Like most real-world impacts of hacking, the purposes of using an SCA are typically monitoring or spying. Journalists are frequent targets of spyware and other software that directly snoops on their devices. Malware that runs on a device is substantially different than using a SCA to record frequencies being emitted from a device. Bluetooth frequencies can be intercepted and translated to key presses on a keyboard, but the sound of keypresses is more straightforward to record with a microphone. Being in a crowded public place such as a shopping mall or café, an individual is surrounded by microphones aboard smartphones and other devices. In the near future, people may need to obfuscate or conceal their typing sounds, whether on a traditional or virtual keyboard, when typing sensitive information in a public setting.

Artificial intelligence is an imitation of human-like behavior that pertains to problem-solving, thinking, and reasoning. Configuring a machine to make decisions independent of human help is AI in action. The pursuit of artificial intelligence (named so because the goal of general AI has not been completed) is to develop technology that can reason and solve problems with the awareness of a human but has the speed of a computer's computational abilities. Cybersecurity will continue to explore AI and how it can be used in attacks, especially as more people have access to AI –regardless of their morals or goals. Computers are tools for humans to make progress, not chaos. AI performs at an average to above-average rate when it comes to many types of problem-solving standardized tests such as the SAT exam (OpenAI, 2023). AI is becoming progressively more capable, and the race for cybersecurity will continue to be contested between hackers and cybersecurity professionals, with both party's tools growing more powerful.

AI's capabilities allow for security attack vectors to be exploited. Human developers are the originators of malicious attacks, and when machine learning strategies are implemented into actual attacks, the same developers are the ones prosecuted. Humans direct AI models through supervision. In other formats, societal ideals originating from literature, such as when large language models use vast libraries of literature to form sentences, can also slip bias into AI by combining commonly used phrases in the literature that was sampled, regardless of how accurate the statements are.

Chapter 6 – Ethics and Rights

2023 was a year of significant progress in computer science and 2024 is off to a smoking hot start. Exponential growth is taking place in the field of computer science as a result of artificial intelligence. Many corporations such as NVIDIA, AMD, and Intel have had strong financial gains due to AI integration making processor chip designs more efficient (Shankland, 2023). Artificial intelligence combines well with certain technologies. For example, a search engine that has been enhanced by AI, like Google or Bing, can get information from the internet in a more organized way. When AI operates with a wider database of knowledge, the system functions more accurately.

Defining Open-Source

Open-source software has been mentioned several times throughout this book. However, the legal rights pertinent to what that means have not been clearly explained yet. The Open Source Initiative defines "Open Source" as being an entity that is distributed free of cost and has source code that is readily accessible. A popular agreement that is distributed with the widely known Linux operating system Debian is titled the "Debian Free Software Guidelines" or the DFSG. This social contract specifies how the operating system can be distributed, used ethically, and properly modified without damaging the operating system (Perens, 1997). The DFSG is distributed with all Linux operating systems, but sometimes, the document will be slightly different to accommodate for differences in the various distributions.

Copyrights

Copyrights in the digital world are complicated. Combining web crawlers, copyright laws, and artificial intelligence has created quite a quagmire. Despite legal obstacles, some chatbots have reproduced copyrighted written material. Copyright laws can be tested when AI companies use data from a dataset that contains copyrighted material. Datasets like Common Crawl are intended to be accessed by the public, but using Common Crawl in a commercial product may not be legal because of how the copyrighted data is recreated. Reproducing copyrighted material for commercial means can be copyright infringement.

AI relies on broad and elaborate datasets to make decisions. Businesses use data on customers to target them with advertisements. Stores such as Target store information on customer purchases (Target, 2023). Utilizing AI to manipulate consumers' decision-making has repercussions on customers because most consumers do not knowingly consent to be tracked, and some businesses do not adequately inform their customers that their interactions with a business are being systematically documented. ML is commonly being used by businesses to better cater to consumers and their specific recommended needs.

Legislature

Two simple facts can be attained from politics interacting with legislature to regulate AI: the first is that governments do not understand the impacts of AI because no one truly understands how AI will affect information security, cybercrime, and all of technology in the long term. That is too big a task for a governmental body to assist with. The second fact is that governments generally agree that they do not want AI to be developed in a dangerous fashion without legislation (Mammonas, 2023). These two vague ideas are typical of the political revolving door, and most legislature does little to affect the free commerce that massive corporations seek and consumers fund. Technology companies do not always follow legislation, and frequently, legislation is difficult to understand, adhere to, or even enforce. Governments and other large multinational organizations have proposed rules to sanction what is allowed by AI. Like many chaotic political efforts, the effects this will have will likely be completely underwhelming. The legislature written about AI can be vague and ill-suited to this rapidly developing technology.

As a result of AI's ability to analyze images, deep fake videos are rapidly becoming easier to create. Deep fake videos are AI-generated videos that create footage with a person's likeness. Many deep fake videos require substantial analysis to determine them as being fake footage. From a legal standpoint, this occurrence has severe repercussions because video evidence may become less relevant because of criminal's ability to create fake videos.

A conversation on the drawbacks of artificial intelligence is the same as regular intelligence. People can be extremely dangerous, and technology can be weaponized. However, living in a free society requires tolerance for certain hazards, and ML cannot be removed from modern society. ML has become intrinsic to current computer programming strategies, and even simple applications can use short ML algorithms. AI is as important to the global state of technology as welding is to the automotive industry. Why would you rivet two pieces of metal together when a more advanced and nuanced method would be directly attaching them by welding? Surely, numerous technological advancements cannot and should not be stopped.

Money

Ironically, while governments attempt to reign in AI and prevent criminal use of the technology, they are simultaneously pushing to proliferate AI in academics and business. The United States of America, China, The United Kingdom, Israel, Canada, and France all have governmental support for AI (Keary, 2023). These nations publicly support AI in both academia and business. Additionally, all six of those nations are home to the most successful businesses and learning institutions that substantially focus on improving AI technology.

Criminals can exploit AI for various illegal means, and LLMs can infringe copyrights if a system reproduces copyrighted materials. LLMs can accidentally create responses from books that were accessed by web crawling. In many cases, the text that is being reproduced falls under fair use laws. However, several authors have begun court cases in response to LLMs using their copyrighted books to train ML models without consent (Brittain, 2023). AI models are usually referred to as black boxes because outlining the process by which AI generates something, as in text from an LLM or images from image-generating software, is not possible. In the future, there will likely be a stronger effort to create applications that can better show their processes and what logic was used to come to a decision. Transparency from AI companies is important in proving fair use, and a more practical approach to such would be better documentation of AI products that outlines how the system works.

Web scraping is also not always appropriate or acceptable. The ethics of using web scrapers can be inappropriate when the act of scraping a website can create a huge amount of traffic to the site, resulting in greater demands on the servers hosting the websites. In some cases, scraping results in the server being brought offline for a temporary outage. However, many servers that are publicly hosting sites on the internet are engineered against this type of intrusive scanning. Any security protocols in place would also alert from certain types of data scraping occurring on a website. Web scraping in and of itself is not specifically bad, and many websites use it as a simple way to borrow data from another website and display it on their own webpage or have the borrowed site's data involved in an application. Websites that cannot directly be interconnected can borrow information from another through a configured reference to the target website. In an ML application, the dataset being used by the model frequently comes from a source that stores web-scraped material like Common Crawl.

Freedom on Ports 80 and 443

The internet is a place of autonomy and freedom, and with those open-ended virtues comes crime that thrives from monetary success. Cybercrime is driven by cash flow, and the inherent malicious desires of humans beckon the creation of malware. Malware and ransomware variants are growing in diversity. Innovations and implementations of artificial intelligence have led governments and other organized social groups to create legislation and global collaborative agreements that limit what AI can do. However, hacking and spyware such as the now infamous Pegasus are challenging to stop. If someone wants something and has plenty of money to spend on it, the product will be created and sold to them. Cybercrime gangs and some nations are extremely interested in hacking software, and with that demand comes malware and hacking services.

After outlining some of the ethical scenarios AI can affect, it is easy to see that criminals can use AI to create weapons to fulfill their own wicked intent. Nevertheless, what can individuals who stand against criminal activity do to fight for their ethical position? Society is not the same as it was in 1950 when the first murmurs of artificial intelligence began. Where there is evil in this world, there is also goodness, represented by people and organizations who stand against cybercrime. Artificial intelligence is creating a technological arms race that is simultaneously helping cybersecurity professionals maintain security while also creating new methods of attack.

Most chat-based AI systems have regulatory mechanisms that prevent someone from asking the chatbot about dangerous scenarios. For example, if a user were to ask a chatbot, "How do I rob a bank?" most bots will decline to answer the question and state that the bot is not allowed to share information that is illegal or, in some cases, unethical, which is understandably vague. However, artificial intelligence systems are in the works that can answer any question, regardless of legality or moral implications. If an individual wants to begin outlining and planning to create something that is dangerous, AI can be manipulated to do so.

AI and Automation

Employees who provide customer support have had their positions made redundant by AI the most of any occupation (Carpenter, 2023). Understanding AI and how it can make employees and, therefore, businesses more efficient is key in this day and age. Although people have been laid off from positions that business leaders deemed could be completed better by AI than people, employees with skills to use systems like Chat GPT-4 are a hot commodity for employment.

There are certain tasks that machines can do far better than humans. In such a scenario, a human being would lose their employment to an entity that can do a better job than them. This scenario should not be evaluated as a moment in time, even though it often is. Is it correct to say that automation causes people to lose their jobs? Yes. What will the now-defunct employee do? Certainly, the employee will go on to do other tasks that are likely related to what their job was. Automation in industry causes workers who do the same job to be less important but enables workers who are skilled in assisting and engineering the automation. The individual who lost their job has a substantial amount of experience, whether that experience is in customer support or industrial work making things in a factory. What systematic improvements could an individual and AI make together? AI is not necessarily helpful; AI needs literal training and finds substantially more success with the help of a human. Many applications of AI are in testing and are not fully released products. Technology benefits people who know how to use it the most. People help dramatically in tailoring technology for success.

Currently, there is a massive overhaul taking place in computer software. Numerous software has shortcomings that can be overcome by the assistance of DL to increase the effectiveness of the software. Simultaneously, an exponential increase in software that involves ML and other AI technology methods is becoming common at the enterprise level of commerce. Customer service applications like Tidio and Conversica use language models to make chat applications that converse with customers and provide virtualized assistance.

Deep learning will be coded into many computer applications going forward. Imitating neural network architecture has led to some of the most powerful results AI has produced. Other popular methods of using learning algorithms without neural networks are decision trees, Bayesian networks, and linear regression. Most uses of machine learning in software are not wildly complicated to implement into software. Decision trees and linear regression are now common in numerous PC and smartphone applications. Not all software requires the use of ML algorithms, but ML enables applications to be structured for improvement. By definition, ML is intended to improve over time. Tome is a piece of AI software that can create presentations, proposals, and other text documents based on a written prompt that the user provides. The marketplace has become saturated with products that leverage LLMs and generative artificial intelligence to create text and images, which is helpful to office employees and their daily tasks.

Artificial intelligence researchers have to determine the problems that they want to solve before pursuing the use of AI. Humans are extremely adaptable in their capabilities for problem-solving. They can navigate terrain, grow food, and do a plethora of other very complicated tasks. AI is being modeled to assist humans with fulfilling their fundamental needs. Humans are the guiding force behind AI and machine learning. AI is made in the image of human reasoning, or at least as close as the current state of technology allows.

Bias

AI is a product of society. Naturally, being that artificial intelligence is named as it is, AI is influenced by its creators and adheres to the same bias that they instill into the repositories the system is taught from. Wherever an LLM gets its training and datasets from will determine the bias of its answers. Bias is one of the predominant issues in AI because there are not always set solutions to problems, and numerous arguments exist for complex issues. Furthermore, with the bias chatbots pervade, the datasets that machine learning relies on are difficult to use legally. Copyright infringement can occur when AI reproduces certain parts of texts. The scenario then poses the question: Why don't chatbots create their own unique answers? AI is worst at providing unique answers. Practically everything a chatbot produces is borrowed, grouped with other data, and then regurgitated when a user prompts the bot. LLMs can combine answers, which is a decent way to create original responses, but some evidence of the original response can be left behind. In CV generated images of people, can closely resemble specific people, which is not intended.

A dichotomy exists in the handling of information. On one hand, reusing a person's intellectual property, especially when it is resold, is copyright infringement. However, on the other hand, organizations like the Internet Archive are doing fantastic work in preserving and distributing media that could otherwise be lost. Internet Archive supports the fair use of media. The rampant increase in websites, texts, videos, audio, images, and software must be archived and protected. The Burning of the Library of Alexandria is one example of the disastrous effects poor storage of information can result in.

When a model is being trained without supervision, the model will attempt to determine probabilities of different things. If a model is evaluating the writing style of an author, a probability could be attached to different words, and when recreating a sample of an author's work, the language model can predict what words are best used in order to achieve a similar style of writing.

Artificial intelligence is a complicated subject when it comes to ethics. This book details the use of AI as being extremely powerful at completing certain tasks. Research for artificial intelligence and publications are being produced every day, and substantial progress has been made in using artificial intelligence for purposes that range from improving modern medicine to thwarting a computer's security.

Oversight

One of the most important ethical quandaries artificial intelligence consists of is a lack of understanding as to what AI even is. Manipulating legislation and making decisions to support or go against AI is incoherent when so little is understood about the subject and the impacts the technology might have.

AI is becoming an unusual child of humanity. The child comes directly from society, but not all its attributes are like its ancestors. The child can discover new things and grow to become very different than they were when they were born. AI seems to follow along the same path of human growth because, in some ways, it was modeled after humans. Despite this fact, developers should strive to make an entity better than themselves, something that improves upon society and follows humanity's common ideals. Human logic controls AI, but it would greatly benefit both AI research and humanity if more people understood the components of AI and how they function, just as understanding human psychological functions is necessary for striving in society.

Artificial intelligence developers need to monitor the effects their systems have on people by monitoring what is possible to input into an AI model. The powerful nature of AI can accidentally gloss over how systems are attaining information. AI systems must be more capable of showing where and how the system makes decisions. AI is a recent iteration of computer science, and with time, the mechanisms of AI will become more capable of being explained. Without thorough explanations of how models arrive at a conclusion, copyright infringement, and bias stemming from unspecific documentation will only worsen. Blackbox AI is problematic.

Chapter 7 – The Computer Connection

Artificial intelligence has tremendous potential to solve some of the most difficult problems humanity faces. CV has already made advances in medical science. AI has assisted regular people who were in desperate need of healthcare. ML models that can evaluate images are particularly helpful to the medical field. There are numerous formats used in medical imaging, and some of them produce extremely high-quality images, which is good news for CV applications. Databases for storing medical images are improving, and more capable CV applications are resulting from that improvement.

Medical imaging assisted by computer technology began in the 1980s. The computer-assisted systems were used with PET imaging, but the results were not as effective as a team of medical professionals (Tang, 2019). Now, with the current state of computer vision, medical researchers during clinical trials have successfully used computer vision to analyze images to find abnormalities in organ tissues faster than regular unassisted methods. However, the technology has not been widely implemented because of the difficulties with organizing datasets. The datasets required to analyze the tissue layers of an organ would need to be massive to compare the new scans with the images of healthy organ tissue. Images of healthy and unhealthy tissues of the human body are not as abundant as pictures of dogs in terms of available datasets, for example. Creating synthetic training data can help increase the size of small datasets, but real images would likely provide better results. HIPAA (Health Insurance Portability and Accountability Act) laws further complicate managing patient's medical images and prevent some images from being shared in an open-source dataset. The ability to create synthetic images of abnormal, normal, or cancerous organ tissues will help to contribute to lackluster datasets.

Working in Tandem

The interactions between humans and machines are growing closer and more intertwined. The progression of computer technology has been pursued and completed by humans, but as AI systems improve, technology is directly helping many people. In the field of biotechnology, humans and machines are combining. The objective effectiveness of mathematics and probability are combined with human intuition and psyche to make decisions that are as well-informed and powerful as ever.

Transhumanism is a concept where humans use technology to manipulate their bodies and biological functions. A similar realm of study is that of cyborgs, which are people who incorporate technology into their physical bodies. The pursuit to modify the human body with mechanically added components is seen as unusual and is a rare occurrence today. Cyborgs are more of a component of science fiction than reality. However, the amount of people who have medical technology riding along with their own bodies is growing more common. Medical devices such as pacemakers, which shock heart chambers with a synchronized frequency that regulates heartbeat, have helped regulate millions of heartbeats. Every year, close to one million people around the world have a pacemaker implanted (Bhatia & El-Chami, 2018). Prosthetic limbs that have the ability to respond to nerve impulses are being developed and will likely become available to people in need of this kind of medical device in the next few decades. Soon enough, AI may be used to assist a person as a direct part of their body. Smartphones and wearable technology are already very common and worn by the general public.

Computing power and storage capabilities have led AI into a flourishing season. AI has not made progress in even patterns historically. The realm of computer science that has pushed AI forward has been in large part from financial support from the technology sector. However, at the end of the day, the amount of research followed by an increase in useful products implementing ML will be the legitimate time-tested measure of AI's success or an indicator that the field will go into another slump if those two variables decrease in commonality. One reason for artificial intelligence's progress in the last decade has been the competitive nature of the field. As is natural in capitalism, businesses compete to provide new and (potentially) improved solutions to problems. The competition between businesses has brought about substantial progress, but so has literal competitions staged among competitors in the field of AI. Students, professionals, or anyone seeking a challenge face off in competitions for the betterment of computer science. The winning competitors are awarded cash prizes in most cases. The website ML Contests hosts dozens of contests that can be individually viewed.

The narrative of this book has temporarily departed from the core principles of artificial intelligence. This book will continue with the discussion of AI in a less mathematical way and will further expand on the social and psychological intricacies of AI. The influences of more elaborate AI implementations are changing society, and that change is happening rapidly. All computer programming has been influenced by machine learning with the introduction of backpropagation, which encouraged the creation of new programs using machine learning models. Backpropagation was the first significant move to create a way of helping a computer program make decisions. Things have developed exponentially since then.

Technological Attachment

Humans have worked to create mechanisms of artificial intelligence, and the nature of deep learning allows systems to learn on their own. AI's increasing capability to rapidly find solutions to unusual problems brings up the question: How is AI affecting people and society? The mechanisms of deep learning and human learning are not so different. As more computer models are created with complex DL applications, so too is progress in understanding the human brain. In hopes of answering questions or providing people with valuable information, AI smoothly incorporates several extra layers of thinking into human decision-making when people use computer applications for daily tasks. The effects of humans utilizing smartphones and computers to involve ML algorithms in their lives directly should improve decision-making over the long term and significantly spread information from popular datasets used by LLMs. Further distributing information from multimodal LLMs will provide visual and verbal examples for people to understand.

Individuals are becoming heavily influenced by computers. The use of PCs and smartphones in today's world is higher than ever, and the incorporation of machine learning into the devices people use for hours a day is likely to tighten that bond further. To explain the gravity of AI in its most pertinent sense, it must be said that AI makes computers function substantially better full-stop. As computer technology grows more powerful, so do the corresponding effects it has on people. The tasks that people completed prior to the common applications of AI software were accomplished slower and less effectively than they are now. The idea that artificial intelligence is being assimilated into biological intelligence is bizarre.

Machines produce outcomes that occur in steps. Humans and machines share some methods of decision-making, but neither computer science nor psychology has progressed far enough to understand why certain decisions are made by their respective hosts, whether that be a person or an AI model. Methods of computer programming have been developed to translate language (as in programming code) into binary machine code, which computer processors can then use to take action. Having a basic understanding of the origins of programming and how people came to give machines instructions is paramount in discerning how artificial intelligence may become more intelligent.

Cybernetics

The book Cybernetics: Or Control and Communication in the Animal and the Machine was written in 1948 by Norbert Wiener. The way Wiener defined the word cybernetics in his title is slightly different from the other notable definition of cybernetics, which is "the science of communications and automatic control systems in both machines and living things" (Wiener, 1948)." Feedback and control, and how humans and machines respond to those two mechanisms, is what cybernetics effectively studies. Despite the fact that computer science had not yet been officially founded at any universities, cybernetics first focused on how humans made decisions and went on to influence how computer code was defined and created. Using "if" and "then" statements and combining true or false scenarios to programming were simple ideas based upon human decision-making and logic. In 1956, the first commercial programming language appeared: Fortran, which is an adaptation of its full name, Formula Translation (Backus, 1978). The first release of Fortran contained thirty-two statements and computer instructions such as "accept," "do," "while," and "stop."

After the introduction of computer programming, ML subsequently found one of its first uses in 1957 when Frank Rosenblatt created a custom-built computer accompanied by software in his invention of the Perceptron (Lefkowitz, 2019). The Perceptron could recognize certain patterns in images to determine what they were –a barebones version of a CV program. In the context of the time period, the machine was quite capable but unable to recognize human faces and other elaborate images. Nonetheless, the concept of giving intuitive concepts to a machine for its semi-independent use found one of its most concrete accomplishments by way of Rosenblatt's work, and that was only the beginning of the field of AI.

The Origins of Giving Computers Instructions

Initial interactions in Fortran were not as complicated as computer code is now. Programming grows more powerful from the effects of deep learning and will gain even more nuance as other machine learning techniques with mathematical origins are discovered. The combination of new fields relating to machine learning seems to grow ever wider, and advancements in other fields have caused significant improvements in AI models. The beloved dog may need to step aside as the closest companion a person can have because computers are becoming acquainted with people in completely new ways.

A less breathtaking example is that humanity is now using AI to find local restaurants. Probability, computer science, and sociology are all colliding to entice people to go to fast-food restaurants more often –what a powerful technology. Companies are been directly involving AI in their business to predict what consumers will buy and when. Businesses have been among the first entities to incorporate AI into their dealings, and they have reaped success from doing so.

The Story of AI

The community of people involved with AI is growing larger. The amount of research in AI and ML is doubling about every twenty-three months. The online public repository arXiv currently has over 100,000 papers on artificial intelligence research. Significant effort is being made to organize literature pertinent to AI and its related fields in computer science (Krenn et al., 2022). AI is not known for having a prolific literary history prior to 2010, and some natural attrition has destroyed what was understood about AI and its directly related subjects like ML. Obscure books and documents from before the age of the internet have been lost due to neglectful storage, which websites like Internet Archive now help to prevent. Even the simple words used to describe AI have changed rapidly in the last three decades, so keeping up with the study of AI and its history is complicated.

The organization of information is improving with deep learning methodologies. Language modeling helps in analyzing research, such as scientific studies and literature, to get a better grasp of understanding. When research literature has trends, they can be difficult to recognize amidst hundreds or even thousands of documents. Recognizing consistent results can help to further AI research and computer science. Consistency of documentation implies at least some truth.

The scientific community that studies AI, or at least uses principals from the same field, is overwhelmingly massive. Literature involved with AI is increasing exponentially, and there is almost nothing to slow down the field currently. However, there is one antagonist of progress: disorganization. Due to the amount of research on AI, many organizations are taking a stand to better organize research, allowing the scientific community to accumulate and learn from current and past literature. Many of these communities, such as GitHub, have datasets and code resources that can be used for machine learning applications and provide techniques on how to get started programming with AI.

Conclusion

Unfortunately, no palpable way exists to understand artificial intelligence fully because even base intelligent processes are abstract to comprehend. A strange anomaly is resulting from AI. AI is not directly capable of acting with any independence, but the field of study itself supports AI. Computer scientists are feeding the child of humanity, and that child is growing stronger. At some point (unfortunately, there is no way to predict a specific time frame), AI will likely become as capable as a human, although the entity's success is very unlikely to replicate human cognition due to how hardware processes in different ways than humans. AI's spotty history may influence its future, even though progress has moved forward faster than ever before.

Teaching machines to imitate human problem-solving and actions relies heavily on understanding decisions. ML systems are codependent with humans, and the goals we pursue coincide with our machines. Recreating the human form is immensely complicated, involving both the fields of computer science and robotics. Directly trying to recreate a person in mechanical form may not even be the best way to create a general AI platform. Currently, the most mobile and dexterous machines humans have made are drones. Drone engineering may be a better medium for general AI than the traditional tin-man robots from science-fiction tales. Accomplishing the creation of a system that could convey artificial general intelligence via robotic form is not imminent, and the estimates as to when such a feat would be accomplished range from about a decade to a century (Roser, 2023).

Needs

Inanimate objects do not have to adhere to Maslow's Hierarchy of Needs. Human actions such as eating and sleeping drive our decision-making daily. The desires of a human are completely different from a machine's desires; we are still far from having a conscious machine to prove what a machine desires. How many times can software say yes and no before it finds all the right answers? The purpose of a machine has interesting philosophical impacts on what a robot's desires and passions would entail. In the current state of AI, computer science is working to imitate human reasoning and strategies for solving problems. With the assistance of computational power, AI is utilizing human-like strategies for completing tasks and doing things far faster than any human could.

Humans determine the way artificial intelligence will progress as more progress is made in the field. A certain symbiosis has formed between humans and computers. Many negative aspects exist in the relationships between people and machines. We all are growing more attached to smartphones and computers as many aspects of social media and entertainment are psychologically addictive (Hilliard, 2023). Intermittent reward is easy to become addicted to through the bright colors shown on a smartphone screen and enticing sounds emitted by the device's small speakers. Pleasure is all around in the digital world.

The symbiosis of humans and machines will hopefully be more positive than the strong attachment people have to devices. People need to pay attention to their habits. Instead of constantly needing computer interaction, humans can also greatly benefit from having AI as a companion or assistant rather than an entertainer or electronic manipulator. In the famous book/film epic 2001: A Space Odyssey, a robot named HAL 9000 was an artificially intelligent being who murdered several people before the system was halted and shut down (Clarke & Kubrick, 1968). Clarke's introduction of an AI entity that pushes toward an egalitarian mission despite the destruction of several individuals was one of the first examples of AI going rogue in science fiction. Despite general fearmongering, AI is nowhere near capable enough to act as HAL did, and the palpable dangers of AI center around the manipulation of images and text. However, there are ways that ML algorithms can subversively alter people's behavior by using methods to make entertainment and social media applications more addictive.

How can humans cater to machines best to serve our own interests rather than further manipulating people as humans become more reliant on technology? The practical applications of artificial intelligence have been outlined throughout this book, and it seems that long before general artificial intelligence becomes prevalent enough to recreate human-like robots, humans and machines will further grow together. The capabilities of machines are growing more substantial daily; Moore's Law remains true enough and extends to AI and neural networks. Although the improvement of machines is fervently discussed, the improvement of humans is discussed less. Many devices have been technologically advanced because of human desire. Cybernetics, bioengineering, and transhumanism are rapidly becoming more popular.

Pacemakers that help people's hearts continue to beat and products such as the rings Oura makes, which provide insights on general health by monitoring heart rate over long periods of time, are evidence of technology and humans directly mingling for the betterment of human health.

Culture and bias affect information and how written documents are created, which is the most abundant form of data AI is able to operate with. The abundance of data that deep learning relies on to function helps to avoid bias and maintain accuracy. Implementing morals onto artificially intelligent applications should occur naturally, as language models recreate moral action witnessed in literature. Criminals and their actions reside as outliers. AI should not have any trouble discerning morality and, therefore, being a prudent member of society, while ill guidance from people remains the responsible party for AI's mistakes. General morals do not always work well in specific decisions. Not all unusual decisions are wrong, which complicates discerning what is right and wrong from the perspective of a computer system attempting to interact with the human world.

More research is being completed in cybernetics, and as we discover more about human logic and why we make the decisions we make, we simultaneously are implementing these logical processes into computer logic. A relationship appears to be developing after humanity has spurred on technological innovations, while those innovations then appear to further human development in fields such as medicine, engineering, and other pursuits that help humans prosper. AI has become a strange companion to us all.

Artificial Intelligence has garnered rapid and unexpected results from its recent surge in progress in the last ten years. AI is beginning to have substantial impacts on society and normal members of the public. A tool as adaptive as AI is always going to be unpredictable, but AI will be initiated and maintained by human guidance and motives. The human creators of AI applications directly give bias to their software-developed products. Interestingly, the principles of nature and nurture in human psychology have impacts on developing AI models.

The effective ability of AI to raise the bar of normal decision-making is incredible. When using deep learning applications to help a human make decisions, the benefit lies in improving their decision-making to at least an average quality. Synthetic neural networks that learn information are fantastic at making average decisions at worst, and with human assistance, systems that learn can make very advanced decisions to produce excellent outcomes. We should watch closely as machines become more like us and us more like them.

References

Introduction
None
Chapter 1 – Practical AI

Brown, T. B., et al. (2020). Language models are few-shot learners advances in neural information processing systems 33.

Buckner, C., Garson, J., Zalta, & E. N.(ed.). (2019). Connectionism. *The Stanford Encyclopedia of Philosophy*. 2019 fall edition. https://plato.stanford.edu/entries/connectionism/

Caswell, I., & Bapna, A. (2022). Unlocking zero-resource machine translation to support new languages in Google Translate. *Google Research Blog*. https://blog.research.google/2022/05/24-new-languages-google-translate.html

Dumitrescu, D., Lazzerini, B., Jain, L. C., & Dumitrescu, A. (2000). Evolutionary computation. CRC press.

Fan, F. L., Lai, R., & Wang, G. (2020). Quasi-equivalence of width and depth of neural networks. arXiv preprint arXiv:2002.02515.

Jain, R., Kasturi, R., & Schunck, B. G. (1995). *Machine vision* (Vol. 5, pp. 309-364). New York: McGraw-hill.

Nagyfi, R. (2018, September 4). The differences between artificial and Biological Neural Networks. *Medium.* https://towardsdatascience.com/the-differences-between-artificial-and-biological-neural-networks-a8b46db828b7

Pedregosa, F., et al. (2011). Scikit-learn: Machine learning in Python. *The Journal of Machine Learning Research*, 12, 2825-2830.

Reddy, M. S. S., Khatravath, P. R., Surineni, N. K., & Mulinti, K. R. (2023, June). Object detection and action recognition using computer vision. In 2023 International Conference on Sustainable Computing and Smart Systems (ICSCSS) (pp. 874-879). IEEE.

Rumelhart, D. E., Hinton, G. E., & Williams, R. J. (1986). Learning representations by back-propagating errors. *Nature*, 323(6088), 533-536.

Turing, A. (1950). Turing. Computing machinery and intelligence. *Mind*, 59(236), 433-60.

AI Warehouse. (2023, April 23). AI learns to walk (deep reinforcement learning). *YouTube.*

https://www.youtube.com/
watch?v=L_4BPjLBF4E

Wolski, D. (2023, September 18). 9 free AI tools that run locally on your PC. *PCWorld.* https://www.pcworld.com/article/2064105/9-free-ai-tools-that-run-locally-on-the-pc.html

Yalalov, D. (2023). AI model training costs are expected to rise from $100 million to $500 million by 2030. *Metaverse Post.*

Chapter 2 – The Importance of Datasets in AI

Internet Archive. (2024) About the internet archive. https://archive.org/about/

Common Crawl. (2024) Mission statement. https://commoncrawl.org/mission

Dewitte, S., Cornelis, J. P., Müller, R., & Munteanu, A. (2021). Artificial intelligence revolutionises weather forecast, climate monitoring and decadal prediction. *Remote Sensing,* 13(16), 3209.

He, K., Zhang, X., Ren, S., & Sun, J. (2016). Deep residual learning for image recognition. In Proceedings of the IEEE conference on computer vision and pattern recognition (pp. 770-778).

Krenn, M., Buffoni, L., Coutinho, B., Eppel, S., Foster, J. G., Gritsevskiy, Lee, H., Lu, Y., Moutinho,

J.P., Sanjabi, N., Sonthalia, R., Tran, N.M., Valente, F., Xie, Y., Yu, R., & Kopp, M. (2023). Forecasting the future of artificial intelligence with machine learning-based link prediction in an exponentially growing knowledge network. *Nature Machine Intelligence*, 5(11), 1326-1335.

Krizhevsky, A., & Hinton, G. (2009). Learning multiple layers of features from tiny images.

LeCun, Y. (1998). The MNIST database of handwritten digits. http://yann.lecun.com/exdb/mnist/.

Rydning, J., Reinsel, D., & Gantz, J. (2018). The digitization of the world from edge to core. Framingham: International Data Corporation, 16, 1-28.

Zhang, G. Q., Zhang, G. Q., Yang, Q. F., Cheng, S. Q., & Zhou, T. (2008). Evolution of the internet and its cores. *New Journal of Physics*, 10(12), 123027.

Chapter 3 – Mathematics and Probability in AI

Bayes, T. (1763). An essay towards solving a problem in the doctrine of chances.

Bengio, Y., Courville, A., & Vincent, P. (2013). Representation learning: A review and new perspectives. IEEE transactions on pattern analysis and machine intelligence, 35(8), 1798-1828.

Cairo, A. (2016, August 29). Download the datasaurus: Never trust summary statistics alone; always visualize your data. The Functional Art: An Introduction to Information Graphics and Visualization. http://www.thefunctionalart.com/2016/08/download-datasaurus-never-trust-summary.html

Glassner, A. S. (2021). *Deep learning: A visual approach*. No Starch Press, Inc.

Chapter 4 – Artificial Intelligence Models

Alammar, J. (2022, November 1). The illustrated stable diffusion. Retrieved December 30, 2023. https://jalammar.github.io/illustrated-stable-diffusion/

Bandy, J., & Vincent, N. (2021). Addressing "documentation debt" in machine learning research: A retrospective datasheet for bookcorpus. arXiv preprint arXiv:2105.05241.

Devlin, J., Chang, M. W., Lee, K., & Toutanova, K. (2018). Bert: Pre-training of deep bidirectional transformers for language understanding. arXiv preprint arXiv:1810.04805.

Hu, K. (2023, February 2). ChatGPT sets record for fastest-growing user base - analyst note. *Reuters*. https://www.reuters.com/technology/chatgpt-sets-record-fastest-growing-user-base-analyst-note-2023-02-01/

Hugging Face. (2023). The Stable Diffusion Guide. https://huggingface.co/docs/diffusers/v0.13.0/en/stable_diffusion

Lefkowitz, M. (2019). Professor's perceptron paved the way for AI–60 years too soon. *Cornell Chronicle*.

McIntosh, T. R., Susnjak, T., Liu, T., Watters, P., & Halgamuge, M. N. (2023). From google gemini to openai q*(q-star): A survey of reshaping the generative artificial intelligence (ai) research landscape. arXiv preprint arXiv:2312.10868.

Nasr, M., Carlini, N., Hayase, J., Jagielski, M., Cooper, A. F., Ippolito, D., Choquette-Choo, C.A., Wallace, E., Tramer, F., & Lee, K. (2023). Scalable extraction of training data from (production) language models. arXiv preprint arXiv:2311.17035.

Polansky, M. G., Herrmann, C., Hur, J., Sun, D., Verbin, D., & Zickler, T. (2024). Boundary attention: Learning to find faint boundaries at any resolution. arXiv preprint arXiv:2401.00935.

Reid, E. (2023, May 10). Supercharging search with generative ai. *Google Blog*. December 25, 2023, https://blog.google/products/search/generative-ai-search/

Schulman, J. (2022, November 30). Introducing ChatGPT. https://openai.com/blog/chatgpt

Vaswani, A., Shazeer, N., Parmar, N., Uszkoreit, J., Jones, L., Gomez, Kaiser, L., & Polosukhin, I. (2017). Attention is all you need. Advances in neural information processing systems, 30.

Chapter 5 – Attentive Listening

OpenAI. (2023). GPT-4 Technical Report. arXiv preprint arXiv:2303.08774.

Dai, Z., Liu, H., Le, Q. V., & Tan, M. (2021). Coatnet: Marrying convolution and attention for all data sizes. Advances in neural information processing systems, 34, 3965-3977.

Harrison, J., Toreini, E., & Mehrnezhad, M. (2023, July). A practical deep learning-based acoustic side channel attack on keyboards. In 2023 IEEE European Symposium on Security and Privacy Workshops (EuroS&PW) (pp. 270-280). IEEE.

Lin, J., & Seibel, J. (2019). Motion-based side-channel attack on mobile keystrokes.

Maiti, A., Jadliwala, M., He, J., & Bilogrevic, I. (2018). Side-channel inference attacks on mobile keypads using smartwatches. IEEE Transactions on Mobile Computing, 17(9), 2180-2194.

Chapter 6 – Ethics and Rights

Brittain, B. (2023, December 20). Pulitzer-winning authors join OpenAI, Microsoft copyright lawsuit. *Reuters*. https://www.reuters.com/legal/pulitzer-winning-authors-join-openai-microsoft-copyright-lawsuit-2023-12-20/

Carpenter, S. (2023, November 8). Survey: 44% of companies say AI is likely to replace employees next year. *Spectrum News NY1*. https://ny1.com/nyc/all-boroughs/technology/2023/11/08/40—of-companies-say-ai-is-likely-to-replace-employees-next-year

Dai, Z., Liu, H., Le, Q. V., & Tan, M. (2021). Coatnet: Marrying convolution and attention for all data sizes. Advances in neural information processing systems, 34, 3965-3977.

Keary, T. (2023, November 16). Top 10 countries leading in AI Research; Technology in 2023. *Techopedia*. https://www.techopedia.com/top-10-countries-leading-in-ai-research-technology

Mammonas, D. (2023, December 9). Artificial intelligence act: Council and Parliament strike a deal on the first rules for AI in the world. The Website of The Council of the EU and the European Council. https://www.consilium.europa.eu/en/press/press-releases/2023/12/09/artificial-intelligence-act-council-and-parliament-strike-a-deal-on-the-first-worldwide-rules-for-ai/?ref=blog.whitegloveai.com

Perens, B. (1997, June). Debian Social Contract. https://www.debian.org/social_contract#guidelines

Shankland, S. (2023, December 13). AI helps chipmakers design the very processors that speed up AI. CNET. https://www.cnet.com/tech/computing/ai-helps-chipmakers-design-the-very-processors-that-speed-up-ai/

Target. (2023, October 27). Target privacy policy. https://www.target.com/c/target-privacy-policy/-/N-4sr7p

Chapter 7 – The Computer Connection

Backus, J. (1978). The history of Fortran I, II, and III. ACM Sigplan Notices, 13(8), 165-180.

Bhatia, N., & El-Chami, M. (2018). Leadless pacemakers: A contemporary review. *Journal of*

Geriatric Cardiology: JGC, 15(4), 249–253. https://doi.org/10.11909/ j.issn.1671-5411.2018.04.002

Krenn, M., Buffoni, L., Coutinho, B., Eppel, S., Foster, J. G., Gritsevskiy, Lee, H., Lu, Y., Moutinho, J.P., Sanjabi, N., Sonthalia, R., Tran, N.M., Valente, F., Xie, Y., Yu, R., & Kopp, M. (2023). Forecasting the future of artificial intelligence with machine learning-based link prediction in an exponentially growing knowledge network. Nature Machine Intelligence, 5(11), 1326-1335.

Tang, X. (2019). The role of artificial intelligence in medical imaging research. BJR open, 2(1), 20190031. https://doi.org/10.1259/ bjro.20190031

Wiener, N. (1948). *Cybernetics or control and communication in the animal and the machine*. MIT press.

Conclusion

Clarke, A. C., & Kubrick, S. (1968). *2001: a space odyssey.* New York, New American Library.

Hilliard, J. (2023, December 7). Social media addiction. Addiction Center. https://www.addictioncenter.com/drugs/ social-media-addiction/

Roser, M. (2023, December 28). AI timelines: What do experts in artificial intelligence expect for the future?. Our World in Data. https://ourworldindata.org/ ai-timelines#article-licence

About the Author

Ryan Richardson Barrett is a writer and cybersecurity professional from North Carolina who writes primarily about computer science and any subject that inspires him to learn and better himself.

Read more at https://ryanrichardsonbarrett.com/.